Cooking with
Fresh Herbs

MAIGA WERNER

Cooking with Fresh Herbs
Green Energy for the Four Seasons

h.f.ullmann

Contents

Preface

People frequently ask me when my involvement with herbs first began, and I think I have finally found the answer to this question: the photo on the left speaks for itself. Even as a small child, I was passionate about gardening, and I feel so lucky that I have always been able to indulge this passion. Thanks to my parents' large garden in the Hunsrück region of Germany, which after several decades was eventually designated a natural herb garden, I was able to cultivate various vegetables and herbs while studying for my degree. Since I never lost my fascination with herbs, a subject which eventually became the heart of my career, I would like to introduce you to the world of herbs by taking you on a culinary journey through the seasons of the herbal year.

It goes without saying that I have not acquired my knowledge from nature alone. My favorite books include *Wild Food* by Roger Phillips, *Mon herbier de santé* (a lexicon of herbal plants) by Maurice Méssegué, and an ancient Roman cookbook by a Roman epicurean by the name of Apicius. Furthermore, I also live with my herbs on what was once an ancient Celtic site—something which is not only wonderfully inspiring in itself but offers a particularly exciting opportunity to experience the world of herbs at first hand in the here and now.

Visitors to our natural herb garden and café are able to discover and, above all, taste all this for themselves! People tend to be amazed when they learn how easy it is to cultivate herbs and discover that not only are all the flowers of herbal plants edible but the leaves can be used for culinary purposes all year round. Medicine and herbal remedies tend to err on the side of caution, but actually there is nothing more natural than the use of herbs and wild plants! Given all the scandals surrounding various foodstuffs, I really cannot recommend herbs highly enough. This simple source of green goodness can do far more than merely enhance the food we eat.

Generally speaking, people do not eat an excessive amount of herbs, and modern-day warnings are frequently based on laboratory tests. The substances contained in herbs will vary enormously depending on location, fertilization, soil composition, soil life, and what else is growing nearby. The simple rule of thumb is never to eat too much of any one food over a long period of time. Nature has so many treasures to offer us that we could try a different herb every day.

The author and publishers assume no liability in this respect, and if you are in any way unsure, we recommend that you first seek advice from a doctor or alternative practitioner.

Why look farther afield:

spring herbs

Early spring is the season when an abundance of vigorous new growth begins to appear, banishing the winter cold and encouraging us to put an end to our inactivity. A monotonous or overly rich diet can leave us with a craving for something fresh and new; so what could be more delicious than the simple wild herbs traditionally found in Nine-herb soup or Maundy Thursday soup?

We begin to see the first shoots of bear's garlic, stinging nettles, ground elder, dandelion, sorrel, and cow parsley, all of which know exactly how to harness the first rays of sunshine, the cool spring air, melt water, and the goodness of the earth. Daisies, garlic mustard, salad burnet, sorrel, yarrow, violets, chickweed, and plantain grasses start popping up in the flower beds and the lawn, and whitetop or hoary cress can be found growing in wall crevices or between cracks in stone work.

Late summer is the time to make sowings of corn salad, whitetop, and roadside pennycress, either on the balcony or in the garden or greenhouse. Some types of wild herbs can simply be left to grow unchecked so that they will be ready to enjoy the following spring.

BEAR'S GARLIC a wonderfully aromatic herald of spring *(Allium ursinum) Amaryllidaceae*

Several years ago—to the delight of all my rose bushes—I planted lots of bear's garlic beneath my fruit trees and shrubs. Over the years, I have been able to observe how the bear's garlic has spread among the strawberries and found its way into other unoccupied spaces so that it now shares the shady areas under trees and bushes with ground elder and woodruff.

Known for its delicate garlic flavor, its strong aroma, and its powerful properties, it also helps to counteract some of the effects of daily environmental pollution. Sadly, it always seems that no sooner have you begun to feast on this herb, than it begins to die back! The important thing now is either to pot up all the little seedlings which have sprouted between the other herbs or else transplant them to empty spots beneath shrubs which have so far not been colonized by bear's garlic.

Basic: bear's garlic pesto Makes 3–4 jars (approx. ½ cup (100 ml) each)

3½ oz (100 g) bear's garlic
gen. ¾ cup (200 ml) rapeseed or olive oil
3 tbsp (40 g) toasted almonds, pine nuts, or walnuts
2 pinches salt

Wash and thoroughly dry the bear's garlic, or else pick it so carefully that it does not need washing. Rinse the jars with boiling hot water, then leave to dry completely.

Purée all the ingredients in a food mixer, then spoon the mixture into the prepared jars. Top each one with a little oil, then close the lid tightly.

Savory wild garlic profiteroles

For the profiteroles (choux pastry)
1 cup (¼ l) water
3½ tbsp (50 g) butter
gen. 1 cup (150 g) flour
4 tbsp (30 g) cornstarch
3–4 eggs

For the filling
1 handful of, e.g. bear's garlic, tarragon, or hyssop, finely chopped
1 handful of other herbs, e.g. field garlic, chives, ground elder, narrowleaf plantain, buckshorn plantain, chickweed, cow parsley, stinging nettles, etc., finely chopped
1 cup (250 g) cream cheese
¾ cup (200 g) sour cream
salt, pepper

Pre-heat the oven to 300 °F (150 °C). Bring the water and butter to a boil in a saucepan.

Stir in the flour and cornstarch, and continue stirring until the mixture comes away from the base of the pan in a clump.

Place in a mixing bowl and gradually mix in the eggs.

Place small mounds of the mixture on a baking sheet and bake in the pre-heated oven for approx. 30 minutes. Slice the profiteroles open while still hot, then leave to cool.

Finely chop the herbs, blend the cream cheese and sour cream together and season to taste, then use to fill the profiteroles.

STINGING NETTLE a natural magician

(Urtica dioica) Urticaceae

I am a huge fan of the animalistic stinging nettle! Not only will it burn you on the outside if you gently brush against its leaves, but it also seems to burn up anything inside the body that is unnecessary, toxic, or waste. However robust and undemanding it may seem, it is very susceptible to being burned itself by late frosts or intense sunlight. It does, however, recover quickly, and we can benefit from its collective properties very agreeably.

In the same way that my horses and goats used to love nettle hay during the winter, I, too, love the first tender tips of this powerful herb. As a mulch or composted, it also provides all kinds of nutrients to young plants and is a useful companion plant to have growing next to fruit trees or other shrubs.

The stinging nettle has meanwhile become one of my top-selling herbs. No longer are stinging nettles merely left to grow around the periphery of the garden to attract butterflies, but are allowed to develop into huge clumps in the middle of the orach field for use in our popular nettle soup served in the café.

TIP   *For winter supplies, stinging nettles can be blanched briefly before freezing or dried for use in tea.*

BUCKSHORN PLANTAIN tender, salty, leafy tongues *(Plantago coronopus) Plantaginaceae*

Unfortunately, buckshorn plantain, which favors saline habitats, keeps on disappearing from my Hunsrück garden, and even in the greenhouse I have to keep making fresh sowings if I forget to supply it with the rations of sea salt that it needs.

With its antler-like and extremely crunchy leaves, coupled with a rather sweet and nutty flavor, which it owes to its seaside origins, it is my favorite among the plantains, all of which are edible. The flower buds of plaintains can be preserved like capers and make a delicious and charming delicacy.

TIP   *See caper recipe on page 100.*

DANDELION bittersweet jack-of-all-trades
(Taraxacum officinale) Asteraceae

The dandelion, along with nettles, sorrel, and narrowleaf plantain, is another of man's constant companions. It will grow in virtually any habitat and there is no leaf shape which it would not develop if it were within its power. However robust the dandelion may seem to us, it reacts extremely sensitively to sun or rain, for example. With its roots reaching deep into the ground, the dandelion brings substances to the surface which then benefit the surrounding plants. As in the case of ground elder, I recommend enjoying the fresh early leaves in a salad or using them as an ingredient in soups or pestos. Unopened buds can be preserved like capers and the flowers boiled into a syrup and stored for winter use. However, what I particularly look forward to every year is the first delicate dandelion leaves. I can never have too many on my morning slice of bread at breakfast, or quite simply with boiled potatoes at lunchtime, or in the evening in a salad with stinging nettle dressing! And even by the time the fall arrives, I will still not have tired of picking and enjoying my dandelion leaves.

GARLIC MUSTARD
wayward garlic stand-in
(Alliaria petiolata) Brassicaceae

This delicate garlic-type plant favors lightly shaded damp corners of the garden, ideally hidden behind bigger plants or shrubs. If I try and grow it in rows, it rewards me by growing quickly, dying back, migrating elsewhere, or being eaten by grubs or insects if I fail to water it enough. Consequently, I prefer to roam around the whole garden on the lookout for its shiny round leaves, which can grow as big as saucers in places where it has deigned to naturalize. The delicate mustardy garlic flavor of the leaves, flowers, and young shoots is present all year round provided conditions are not too dry and provided we gardeners tolerate these amazing little plants in our gardens in the first place, recognizing how they co-exist in harmony and partnership with their neighbors.

TIP   *Despite its wayward habit, garlic mustard can still be grown for a while in a pot or window box on a balcony. As with other members of the cabbage family, like whitetop, roadside pennycress, annual and perennial arugula, watercress, or scurvy grass, fresh garlic mustard can be enjoyed all year round. I personally would plant it with parsley and chervil.*

Ré's energy cookies

1⅓ cups (300 g) butter
vanilla extract, to taste
gen. 1 cup (125 g) confectioners' sugar
salt
2 egg yolks
4⅓ cups (500 g) flour
2½ cups (250 g) ground walnuts
1 cup roasted nettle seeds

Pre-heat the oven to 340 °F (170 °C). Beat the butter until creamy, then stir in the vanilla extract, confectioners' sugar, salt, and egg yolks.

Add the flour, walnuts, and nettle seeds, then knead the mixture well. Roll into little balls, press gently onto a greased baking sheet, and shape into little mounds.

Bake in the pre-heated oven for 20 minutes until light golden brown.

TIP   *You can buy stinging nettle seeds in health food stores.*

Wild herb pesto   Makes approx. 5 jars (approx. ½ cup (100 ml) each)

½ cup (80 g) almonds or walnuts
⅓ cup (15 g) dandelion—*bitter, tangy*
scant ⅓ cup (10 g) salad burnet—*nutty*
gen. ⅓ cup (20 g) bear's garlic, garlic mustard or garlic chives—*garlic*
gen. ⅓ cup (20 g) stinging nettles—*juicy and sweet*
gen. ⅓ cup (20 g) narrowleaf plantain or lamium—*mushroom*
gen. ⅓ cup (20 g) common purslane, chickweed or saltbush (garden orach)—*delicate salady, peasy flavor*
gen. ⅓ cup (20 g) sorrel—*tangy*
⅔ cup (30 g) ground elder—*sweet and carroty*
⅓ cup (15 g) comfrey—*cucumber flavor*
¼ cup (10 g) whitetop or pepperweed—*sweet and mustardy to round things off!*
1⅔ cups (400 ml) rapeseed or olive oil
1 tsp (6 g) rock salt, Himalayan salt, or sea salt
pepper, to taste

Wash the jars in boiling hot water, then dry thoroughly.

Briefly toast the almonds or walnuts in a dry skillet, then leave to cool.

Roughly chop the herbs into small pieces, then purée in a food processor or blender with the oil and salt.

Add the nuts, purée, and season to taste. Spoon the mixture into the prepared jars, top up with a little oil, then close the lids tightly.

Two leaves or, ideally, some flowers of ground ivy will add a very special flavor to this pesto.

CREEPING CHARLIE OR GROUND IVY
magical herbal vine
(Glechoma hederacea) Lamiaceae

I always look forward to seeing the prettily aromatic tendrils of ground ivy creeping through the garden in spring and turning into a delicious garland, which will at some point delight us with its lilac flowers. Even with just a few leaves and flowers, this insignificant-looking labiate packs a strong aromatic punch. Its unusual flavor goes well with rich dishes and sauces and lends a very distinctive seasoning to spring soups. I personally find it very appealing to add the flowers to herb-flavored quark or serve the leaves as an accompaniment to dishes based on goat's or sheep's cheese. For if you examine the individual strands of the overall aroma of ground ivy more closely, you will discover a slight hint of sheep or goat.

TIP   *Ground ivy is a crucial ingredient of Nine-herb soup, traditionally served at the start of spring. Its tiny flowers will enhance any spring quark dish and, if it is grown in a container, it spills prettily over the edge of the tub. However, it must be kept in check if grown with other plants as it can easily take over.*

Variation of Nine-herb soup   `VEGAN`

Wash the herbs, drain, then finely chop.

Finely chop the onions and sweat in the oil. Sprinkle with spelt flour, then slowly pour in the vegetable stock, stirring constantly. Bring the soup briefly to a boil, then simmer for about five minutes.

Add the herbs and leave to steep for a few minutes. Sprinkle with daisies and season to taste with herb salt and pepper.

Purée the soup or press through a sieve, as desired. Top with a dollop of soy cream or, if you are not a vegan, with natural cream or crème fraîche.

1 handful each of stinging nettles, bear's garlic or garlic mustard, ground elder, daisies, dandelions, yarrow, chickweed, plantain
8–10 ground ivy leaves
2 onions
2 tbsp olive oil
2 tbsp spelt flour
1 quart (1 l) vegan vegetable stock
pepper, herb salt, nutmeg
soy or natural cream, or crème fraîche

NARROWLEAF OR RIBWORT PLANTAIN
balsamic king of summer *(Plantago lanceolata) Plantaginaceae*

Narrowleaf plantain and its cousins, hoary plantain (*Plantago media*) and broadleaf or common plantain (*Plantago major*), have lots of room in my garden to run wild and establish themselves. Despite the different variations, it is mainly narrowleaf plantain which ends up in my salads and other herbal creations, such as pestos or soups.

If you are plagued in summer by mosquito or other insect bites, just take two to three juicy narrowleaf plantain leaves, rub them briefly between the palms of your hands, and use the juice to relieve the irritated skin. The soothing effect is immediate and lasting. In doing so, you may notice a mushroomy smell coming from the rubbed leaves, which is even more distinct if you chew on the plantain's unopened buds.

TIP *See caper recipe on page 100.*

Narrowleaf plantain and chickpea medallions `VEGA`

1½ cups (250 g) dried chickpeas
vegetable stock, vegan
5 bay leaves
1 tbsp thyme leaves
1 tbsp lovage, chopped
20 narrow plantain leaves, chopped
small amount of spelt flour
salt, pepper, nutmeg, to taste
oil, for frying

Soak the chickpeas overnight.

Cook them in the vegetable stock along with the bay leaves until soft. Remove the bay leaves once the chickpeas are cooked.

Flavour the chickpeas with thyme, lovage, and plantain leaves, purée, then season to taste. Add a little more vegetable stock or spelt flour, depending on consistency.

Shape the mixture into rounds and fry on both sides until golden brown.

TIP *Wild herb salad, herb-flavored quark, wild herb pesto, or beet salad all make excellent accompaniments to this dish.*

SALAD BURNET
slighty acidic, nutty leaves
(Sanguisorba minor) Rosaceae

Salad burnet is an unassuming member of the rose family which loves the company of grasses, a characteristic which makes it rather difficult for us gardeners to harvest its delicate, lacy leaves. If grown in a greenhouse, salad burnet can be harvested almost all year round. It also seems to like the proximity of bulbous plants, such as garlic, garlic chives, onions, bear's garlic, and Welsh onion or Egyptian tree onion. Mixing these bulb plants with salad burnet also helps inhibit the latter's susceptibility to rust damage. As an important aromatic element of green sauce, salad burnet already plays a major role in the kitchen, but the slightly nutty flavor of its delicate leaves also adds an unmistakable note to wild herb pestos or wild herb soup. And last but not least, its lacy, filigree leaves can be used to provide a magical table decoration.

Classic Frankfurt Green Sauce traditionally consists of seven herbs: borage, chervil, (water-)cress, salad burnet, parsley, sorrel, and chives. They are finely chopped, mixed with sour cream and/or homemade mayonnaise, and served with hard-boiled eggs. There are also numerous other versions of this sauce, not just in Germany but around the world, consisting of many different combinations, the origins of which can be traced back to Roman times.

Venison and herb patties

Wash and dry, then finely chop the herbs. Very finely chop the onions, then mix them with the ground meat along with the herbs.

Season the mixture, add the egg and bread roll, then knead all the ingredients together. Shape into patties and fry in a little oil.

herbs (equal in volume to the amount of meat): equal amounts of salad burnet, sorrel, Welsh onion, chives, ground ivy, chervil, narrowleaf plantain
2 large onions
1 cup (250 g) ground venison or other ground meat
salt, pepper, hot mustard
1 egg
1 day-old bread roll, soaked in milk
small amount of Japanese water pepper or chile, finely chopped

SORREL—unfailing source of freshness

(Rumex acetosa and acetosella) Polygonaceae

Sorrel, an unfailing source of freshness, can be found almost all year round, enabling us to harvest it to add to our salads, pestos, or sorrel soup. It is one of the few really well-known herbs which people participating in my seminars remember from their childhood. It goes without saying that my brothers and I also ate it when we were children. Bizarrely, I came across it again when I was a student in Wuppertal and worked part-time as a cook in a bistro. The owner, a Frenchman, always brought big jars of preserved French sorrel back from the wholesalers which I then had to turn into cream of sorrel soup. So, it's always a good idea to preserve a few herbs in lactic acid for the winter (see recipe below). Gardening tip: as well as being a colorful addition to a salad, bloody dock *(Rumex sanguineus)* with its red-veined leaves also makes an attractive plant to place around pond margins or in any semishaded area of the garden.

Basic: preserving herbs by lacto-fermentation **VEGAN**

sorrel
1 tbsp (15 g) sea salt to 1 quart (1 l) water

TIP
Nearly all herbs and vegetables can be stored and combined for winter use using this preserving method.

Bring the sea salt and water to a boil, then leave to cool until lukewam. Wash and carefully dry the sorrel, then chop finely.

Transfer the sorrel to an air-tight sealable jar and top up with salt water, taking care that no air remains in the mixture. Leave about 1 inch (3 centimeters) of space at the top for the fermentation process.

Seal the jar, then stand in a warm place for approx. 8–10 days. When bubbles begin to rise, move the jar to a cooler location. The sorrel will be ready in 2–8 weeks and will keep over winter. This is a good way to store and be able to enjoy your own herbs throughout the winter months.

Sorrel and bean salad **VEGAN**

1½ cups (250 g) dried butter beans/lima beans
vegetable stock
2 large carrots
2 handfuls sorrel, French or Roman or shield-leaf sorrel
1 handful golden raisins
salt, pepper, nutmeg
1 tbsp vinegar
2 tbsp oil
1 tbsp capers

Soak the beans overnight in water. Next day, cook until soft in plenty of vegetable stock. Drain the beans while reserving the stock. Cut the carrots into small pieces, then cook in the stock until soft but still firm. Drain once more, while still reserving the stock. Add the golden raisins to the stock and cook until softened.

Wash, dry, and finely chop the sorrel. Mix the sorrel with the cooled beans, raisins, and carrots. Season to taste with the salt, pepper, vinegar, oil and nutmeg, then sprinkle with capers, to taste.

FRENCH SORREL acid drop
(Rumex scutatus) Polygonaceae

Used instead of an acid drop between flavors or to neutralize the palate during a herb-tasting session, French or shield-leaf sorrel never fails to trigger a "wow" reaction. I found this small sorrel plant in the mountains of Andalusia as well as among the craggy cliffs of the Mosel mountains. It can also be cultivated wonderfully well in your own garden or in pots. If it is provided with enough nutrients and water, it will grow so quickly that it can produce enough growth from week to week, from spring to fall, to enhance our salads with its extremely tangy and decorative leaves. If you pick the leaves regularly, this herb will often keep on growing and spreading as if frequent harvesting encourages extra growth, especially if you always remember to say thank-you to the plants!

TIP   *Since sorrel is totally robust and hardy with no need of protection as well as very deep-rooted, even in gravel, and can spread without becoming rampant, it makes a perfect trailing plant.*

Juicy corn-fed chicken breast stuffed with sorrel butter

Wash the sorrel, then allow to drain in a colander. Purée the sorrel, the lemon juice, and a little salt and pepper together, using a hand-held blender, until the mixture forms a smooth pesto.

Cream the butter and stir in the sorrel pesto, then season to taste with salt and pepper.

Rinse the chicken breasts and pat dry. Lay them skin side down and carefully make a cut part way through the breast to create a pocket.

Pre-heat the oven to 340 °F (170 °C). Spoon the sorrel butter into a piping bag and pipe into the pocket.

Season the chicken breast on both sides with salt and pepper and toss in flour. Heat the oil in a skillet and sauté for approx. 2 minutes on each side. Pierce with a sharp knife to check the juices are running clear.

Cook in the pre-heated oven for 10–15 minutes with the skin uppermost.

4 corn-fed chicken breasts, approx. 7 oz (200 g) each, unskinned
⅔ cup (40 g) French sorrel
⅔ cup (150 g) butter
1 tsp (5 g) lemon juice
2 tbsp flour
1 tbsp oil
salt, pepper

A recipe by Sebastian Schuff

Cod with tomato foam and corn and herb fritters Serves 4

4 portions of cod fillet, 5½ oz (150 g) each

For the herb-flavored oil

1 quart (1 l) olive oil
peel of 1 lemon
2 bay leaves
1 star anise
2 tbsp wholegrain mustard
½ tonka bean
1 tbsp white peppercorns
1 sprig rosemary
3 sprigs thyme
2 leaves Japanese water pepper
2 garlic cloves

For the tomato foam

6 tomatoes
1 bunch of basil
12 sweet dates
3 tbsp olive oil
1 dash white balsamic vinegar
1 dash dark balsamic vinegar
4 sheets of gelatin
¾ cup (200 g) heavy cream

For the corn and herb fritters

1¼ cups (180 g) flour
1 cup (140) polenta, finely ground
¾ oz (22 g) fresh yeast, if using dry follow maker's instructions
1 scant cup (220 ml) milk
1 egg
salt, grated nutmeg
½ bunch each of parsley, French sorrel, and thyme

A recipe by Michael Daus

To make the herb oil, heat all the spices and olive oil together to approx. 176–185 °F (80–85 °C), then leave to stand in a closed container overnight.

The following day, make the tomato foam by peeling and quartering the tomatoes, then scoop out the flesh. Set aside the skins.

Place the tomato flesh and basil in a food processor with just enough water to cover. Purée the ingredients until smooth, then pour into a sieve and allow to drain.

Add the cream to the tomato mixture, then season to taste with white balsamic vinegar, salt, and pepper.

Soak the gelatin according to the instructions on the packet. Heat a small amount of the white "tomato foam" and dissolve the softened gelatin in it. Transfer the tomato foam to an espuma whipper and chill in the refrigerator for 2–3 hours.

To make the corn fritters, combine the flour and polenta. Heat the milk and dissolve the yeast in the warmed milk. Add the egg, then season with salt, pepper and nutmeg. Combine the yeast mixture with the flour and polenta and mix into a smooth dough.

Wash, dry, and finely chop the herbs, then mix into the dough. Leave the dough to stand for approx. 30 minutes. Fry small portions of the mixture in a deep-fat fryer.

Finely chop the tomato skins and dates, then mix with dark balsamic vinegar and olive oil to taste.

Season the cod with salt and pepper, then fry in a skillet with a little oil.

Re-heat the herb oil, this time adding the fresh herbs, to 176–185 °F (80–85 °C) again, add the cod, and cook for approx. 7–8 minutes, taking care to maintain a constant temperature.

Carefully remove the cod, allow to drain for a short while, then serve on a bed of tomato foam. Serve with the corn fritters.

TIP   *The white frothed tomato can easily be turned into white cream of tomato soup. Simply leave out the gelatin and serve the soup hot.*

Goat's cheese medallions caramelized on a bed of herb salad with croutons Serves 4

Wash the salad herbs, then spin dry. Arrange on plates.

Slice the white bread into cubes and sauté in a small amount of the butter until golden brown. Heat the remaining butter, add the herbs, and toss in the hot butter.

Allow the maple syrup to caramelize in a skillet, then add the rounds of goat's cheese.

Season with sea salt and arrange the goat's cheese on a bed of herb salad.

Add a dash of balsamic vinegar and a little olive oil to the caramelized syrup left in the skillet, then thicken with the chilled butter. Drizzle this marinade over the herb salad.

For the goat's cheese medallions
4 rounds of goat's cheese, 3 oz (80 g) each
⅔ cup (150 ml) maple syrup
4 tsp (20 g) chilled butter, cubed
2 tsp sea salt

For the herb salad
1 bunch each of dandelion, arugula, chervil, parsley, bronze fennel,
sweet cicely, French sorrel, orach
white balsamic vinegar
2 tbsp olive oil
salt, pepper

For the herb croutons
4 slices white bread
1 bunch thyme leaves, stripped
2 sprigs finely chopped rosemary
½ bunch chopped parsley
1 garlic clove
⅔ cup (150 g) butter

A recipe by Michael Daus

Sorrel pesto

Wash and drain the sorrel, then chop roughly.

Purée the sorrel with all the other ingredients apart from the salt and lime zest. Then add salt and lime zest to taste.

3 bunches of French sorrel
½ cup (120 ml) sugar syrup
⅔ cup (100 g) pine nuts
scant ½ cup (100 ml) olive oil
salt
zest of ½ lime

A recipe by Sascha Daniels

SCENTED VIOLETS intoxicating harbinger of spring *(Viola odorata) Violaceae*

After the whites and yellows of winter, violets, which provide one of the first colorful splashes of the season, are guaranteed to make your heart sing! Their appearance presages their bewitching scent, which is released in sunlight and is a clear signal that spring has begun.

Meanwhile, these native blue scented violets and their red relatives, which I planted myself, have spread all over the garden, not least thanks to the efforts of industrious ants. They seem to be happy both under the berry bushes and in huge clumps amid the sparse lawn, where they give off their incomparable fragrance on sunny spring days.

The young shoots, leaves, and flowers can be used in salads and sauces or served with vegetables. As with chicory and dandelions, the roots can be roasted as a coffee substitute from fall onward.

I personally love the flowers best, which can be sprinkled over salads, or dried, sugared, candied, or preserved in wine or schnapps to make a delicious aromatic ingredient in chocolates, cakes, ice cream, or sauces. Violets, with their special aroma, inject a particularly delicate note in wild herb pestos.

Sugared violets

50 clean small blue scented violets
1 very fresh egg white
3 tbsp (50 g) superfine sugar

Using a fine, good-quality brush (it must not shed any hairs!), dip the tip into egg white whisked in a porcelain bowl. Brush each flower on both sides with egg white, then dip briefly and gently in sugar. Leave to dry on parchment paper.

TIP *Violets or violet syrup can be used instead of Spanish thyme to flavor panna cotta (see recipe on page 79). In this case, only the flowers and not the leaves should be used.*

SWEET WOODRUFF balsamic sweetness
(Galium odoratum)

Luckily, sweet woodruff ice cream is available once again from the Italian ice cream parlor. Combined with chocolate ice cream, this has become my regular order—with cream, naturally. And the little paper bags rustling mysteriously and containing woodruff sherbet can also still be found occasionally.

Be that as it may, we now conjure up our own woodruff creations for our guests to enjoy in May. As a child, I discovered woodruff among the beech woods of Hunsrück and dug up a few roots of this member of the madder family to plant in our own garden, where it shares the semi-shade amongst the berry bushes with bear's garlic and ground elder. In the meantime, it has spread to such an extent that we can spoil our guests with delicious woodruff specialties.

TIP   *The best way to transplant woodruff in the garden is to transplant the root offshoots to a spot beneath deciduous shrubs and trees. It can be kept as a ground-covering plant in pots at the base of other plants and harvested naturally. I pick woodruff until late in its flowering season. To create various delicacies, such as chocolates, punch, cakes, or ice cream, pick approx. 20 stems, then leave them to dry out for a day, then boil them with sugar to make a syrup.*

Sweet woodruff syrup

Allow the woodruff to dry out, then crush it with a rolling pin. Transfer it to a sealable jar, top up with wine and leave to steep for 3 days.

Drain off the liquid, then boil it in a saucepan with 1 quart (1 liter) of water and a scant ½ cup (100 g) of sugar until it turns into a syrup. Pour it into jars, then seal the lids.

Basic recipe for syrup, see page 99.

Fresh herb tea: Maiga's companion mixture

Mix equal parts of stinging nettles, angelica leaves, lady's mantle, daisies, ground elder, shepherd's purse, rose petals, beebalm, catnip, [rosebay] willowherb, and lemon balm, a little oregano, parsley, rose, rosemary, and yarrow.

TRADITIONAL SCENTED ROSES

Gallic roses, moss roses, alba roses, damask roses, or centifolia roses delight us with their intense, heavy perfume. We have various old varieties growing in our garden, which we continue to cultivate without grafting. Although they do not flower as often as modern roses, they are nevertheless very robust and undemanding. They begin flowering in June, after which not a single day passes when I do not stop beneath the rose arbors to breathe in their different scents.

I collect whole blooms to dry on a drying rack for winter use. I decorate my different teas with rose flowers or use them to make my salves.

I also use fresh roses in cream cakes and in ice cream, syrup, jam, conserves, and sauces.

Rose cream gateau

For the sponge

5 eggs
salt
scant 1 cup (200 g) sugar
gen. 1⅓ cups (200 g) flour
4 tbsp liquid (e.g. milk, water, rose water, juice, or similar)

For the cream cheese filling

2 cups (500 g) whipping cream
2 cups (500 g) quark
scant ½ cup (100 g) sugar, and cream stabilizer, if needed
gen. ¾ cup (200 ml) rose syrup
(Basic recipe for syrup, see page 99)
plenty of fresh rose petals

1 short pastry base
4 tbsp (100 g jam), e.g. rose or quince jelly

Pre-heat the oven to 300 °F (150 °C). Separate the eggs. Whisk the egg white with a little sugar and pinch of salt until stiff. Beat the egg yolks with the remaining sugar until the mixture turns pale and creamy. Stir in a little liquid, then sift in the flour and blend. Carefully fold in the stiff egg white. Pour the mixture into a greased spring-form pan and bake immediately in the pre-heated oven for approx. 25 minutes. Leave to stand in the oven for a short while before removing. Run a knife around the edge of the spring-form to release the sponge, then tip it out onto a wire rack. Once it is cold, slice into 2 or 3 layers.

To make the filling, whisk the cream until stiff. Stir sugar and cream stabilizer, if necessary, into the rose syrup. Add the quark and fold in the whipped cream. Spoon some of the cream into a piping bag for decorating, if desired.

Lay the pastry base on a cake plate, spread with a layer of jam, then place the first sponge layer on top, pressing down gently. Then spread one-third or half of the cream mixture over the top and top with another layer of sponge.

If making a 3-layer cake, spread with half the remaining cream, then top with a third layer of sponge. Spread the rest of the cream over the top of the cake, decorate with fresh rose petals, and chill in the refrigerator until firm.

TIP   *To make a woodruff gateau (see picture on page 32) replace the rose syrup with woodruff syrup (see page 33).*

Under the umbrella of the umbellifer family

The family of umbellifers is by no means unfamiliar in culinary circles: anise, dill, fennel in its various forms, as a tea or as a vegetable, carrots, chervil, caraway and cumin, cilantro, in leaf or seed form, lovage, parsnip, parsley, celery. Over the following pages I will introduce you to a few of the less well-known members of this family.

COMMON HOGWEED subtle seducer

Cow parsnip (Heracleum sphondylium) Apiaceae

It is always so heartening to watch little seedlings begin to sprout after the seeds have been sown and watered. However, I can barely contain my excitement when I see the tiny little shoots of these two classic umbellifers, shaped like a claw-like sheath, begin to emerge! Our native "smaller" common hogweed or cow parsnip is wholly edible and is even credited with aphrodisiac properties. Borscht soup derives its name from *borschtyevik*, the Russian word for hogweed, and the Latin name for giant hogweed, *Heracleum mantegazzianum* (belonging to Hercules), likewise suggests great strength. Its attractive large umbrella-like flowers have a slightly sweet aroma and the seeds hint at a combination of cilantro and lovage. The freshly flowered umbrels taste delicious cooked in pancake batter, the same cooking method traditionally used for elderflower blossoms but with an irresistibly seductive, delicate, savory difference!

Warning   *Skin contact with common hogweed can cause redness of the skin, together with itching and blistering. Always wear gloves when picking common hogweed. Make sure that you do not confuse it with giant hogweed (Heracleum mantegazzianum), as this can cause nasty burns if you touch it.*

Hogweed fritters

Make a pancake batter by blending the milk, flour, eggs, salt to taste, and oil.

Lightly beat the umbrels of hogweed, then dip them in the batter. Fry in a skillet containing plenty of oil and serve sprinkled in confectioners' sugar, if desired.

2 cups (½ l) milk
gen. 1⅓ cups (200 g) flour
3 eggs
salt
oil
approx. 25 hogweed umbrels

TIP   *This dish is traditionally made using elderflower blossom...*

GROUND ELDER deep-rooted sensitivity and strength *(Aegopodium podagraria) Apiaceae*

In France, ground elder is also known as "la petite angélique," i.e. the baby sister of angelica, a name I find rather sweet and very appropriate! However, ground elder is also regarded as an invasive weed and a real nuisance by many gardeners, but we should simply accept with a smile and incorporate—quite literally, i.e. by eating as much as possible—the remarkable strength contained in each little piece of root.

Tasting of tangy carrot and ideal for sweet, hearty dishes, ground elder makes an excellent accompaniment or main dish and features in a wealth of recipe ideas. We could probably fill an entire book with such recipes, but will limit ourselves here to our favorite dishes, including carrot and ground elder cake or ground elder quiche. But see for yourself and try stuffing pasta pockets or ravioli with ground elder! Delicious!

TIP *I always use the first, pale-green leaves while they are still unopened and transparent, cutting back or mowing the entire plant every few weeks to encourage the fresh growth of tender baby leaves.*

Ground elder quiche

For the pastry
1¾ cups (250 g) flour
9 tbsp (130 g) butter
6 tbsp (90 ml) water
½ tsp salt

For the filling
2 handfuls of young ground elder leaves
1 handful each of chopped chives, lovage, herbs of choice
1 cup (250 ml) vegetable stock
1 cup (200 g) sour cream or crème fraîche
3 eggs
salt, pepper
nutmeg

Mix together the flour, butter, water, and salt to make a smooth dough, wrap in foil, then chill in the refrigerator for half an hour. Roll out the pastry and line a prepared spring-form pan. Sprinkle the ground elder and other herbs over the base.

Pre-heat the oven to 300 °F (150 °C). Lightly beat the vegetable stock, sour cream, and eggs together, then season with salt, pepper, and nutmeg. Pour the mixture over the ground elder and herbs and bake for approx. 1 hour in the pre-heated oven until the egg mixture is firm.

BALDMONEY OR BEARWORT feathery
flavoring miracle *(Meum athamanticum) Apiaceae*

You will be amazed when you taste the lovely, subtle flavors of fennel, caraway, and lovage, and when you sample the stunning baldmoney herb for the first time. This thick, bright green, bushy plant, which resembles dill but with more branching stems, can grow unobtrusively upright in the garden for weeks on end. It keeps its umbelliferous flowers well hidden and has so far not provided me with any seeds. Perhaps it does not like the soil or climate in Hunsrück since it originally comes from more mountainous areas, like the Alps or the Scottish Highlands, where it is, or at least used to be, a traditional kitchen herb.

Meanwhile, I have successfully managed to divide my single bearwort plant and I am hoping that I will now be able to harvest a bit more—so that I can indulge my gourmet customers with its amazing range of flavors. There are several types of schnapps called "Bärwurz" (Bearwort), which are indeed made from bearwort as well as from one of its close relatives, mountain lovage (*Ligusticum mutellina*).

Umbel soup with carrots Serves 4

Clean and slice the carrots. Peel and finely chop the ginger.

Sweat the shallots in a little butter or oil until translucent, then add the sliced carrots and ginger. Season with salt and pepper and continue to cook the carrots gently.

Add the water, simmer until the liquid has reduced a little, then pour in the cream and milk. Cook the carrots until tender, then purée all the ingredients in a blender until smooth. Meanwhile, gradually add the olive oil, a little at a time.

Transfer the soup to a saucepan. Wash the herbs, pat dry, and roughly chop. Add them to the soup and bring to the boil once more. Turn off the heat, then leave to infuse for 5–6 minutes.

Pass the soup through a sieve, season with a dash of balsamic vinegar to taste, and serve in soup bowls.

1 lb 2 oz (500 g) carrots
knob of butter
1 piece of ginger
4 shallots, chopped small
salt, pepper
7 tbsp (100 ml) water
scant ½ cup (100 ml) light cream
1¼ cups (300 ml) milk
⅓ cup (80 ml) olive oil
½ bunch each of sweet cicely,
bronze fennel,
ground elder, and chervil
½ cilantro leaf
balsamic vinegar

A recipe by Michael Daus

COW PARSLEY carroty star of the wild

(Anthriscus sylvestris) Apiaceae

Cow parsley, which begins flowering in early May, is one of the many wild herbs which I have never had to cultivate deliberately in the garden. In company with ground elder, stinging nettles, dandelions, narrowleaf plantain, and sorrel, it is a true garden friend which has thrived in this garden since my parents' time when I used to play among it with my toys or guinea pig. In my child's eye, the area where the cow parsley grew was one vast, mysterious fern forest.

Unfortunately, it is easy to confuse this coarse umbellifer with its grooved stem with some of its toxic or inedible relatives. With fool's parsley (*Aethusa cynapium*), for example, an annual weed which grows around the edge of fields and germinates in the garden throughout the summer, quickly coming into flower. Or hemlock (*Conium maculatum*), which I have only ever seen along dry river banks, where it can grow to a height of 6–7 feet (2 meters) or more and flowers from July onward. However, these two poisonous plants have smooth, rounded stems, and hemlock stems are also speckled with red and the plant has either a rather unpleasant smell or none at all. If you have any doubts at all as to whether the plant is cow parsley or not, leave it well alone and buy one instead.

I am always looking at English seed catalogs or herb nurseries in my search for special plants. I once found a very lovely red cow parsley plant called "Raven's Wing," which makes a very ornamental addition to my beds. Its powerful carroty flavor and sturdy leaves, very similar to those of carrots, are in great demand in the restaurant kitchen, not just for decoration but also to add flavor to hearty soups, pestos, and salads.

Herb smoothie with kefir

8–10 cups (300 g) mixed herbs of choice
1 large carrot
1 small cucumber
2 cups (500 ml) kefir
1 tbsp almond butter or blanched almonds
salt
agave syrup or honey
lemon juice, or a little lemon verbena

Begin by washing and drying the herbs, then the carrot and cucumber. Chop everything into small pieces, then purée all the ingredients in a blender.

Add the kefir, almond butter, salt, syrup or honey, and lemon juice to taste, then mix again thoroughly.

TIP   *I always try and sample different herbs individually, but my favorite smoothie is made from a mixture of umbrels, especially ground elder, sweet cicely, and cow parsley. Stinging nettles and a hint of mint also make an excellent combination.*

ANGELICA divine queen of herbs

(Angelica archangelica) Apiaceae

To judge from my own experience with angelica, I have to conclude that snails, instead of being purely destructive, can, on the contrary, actually be very advantageous to a plant's health. Snails once completely devoured an entire group of potted angelica seedlings. Yet a few weeks later, strong, dark-green plants began shooting up from these forgotten pots, never again to be attacked by snails. Despite its majestic height, angelica will find a modest spot even in a small garden where it can unfold its arching leaves. Whether it is used for culinary purposes or not, I just find it so attractive to look at. I sometimes plant it in rows as a screen or simply to admire its angelic appearance. In its first year of growth, it will provide a plentiful supply of leaves, while the stems can be candied and the rest dried for winter tea—my first line of defense against stomach-ache or lethargy. In its second or third year, angelica will produce a large, globe-like umbrel which, if glimpsed out of the corner of an eye, really can make you think there is an angel in the garden.

TIP   *A quick way to make candied angelica is to slice the stalks into sections and cook in sugar syrup. Traditionally, you will need one part each of water and sugar to make sugar syrup. This mixture should be simmered until the sugar is dissolved. Candied angelica is perfect for use in all kinds of goodies like cakes or chocolates, or in jams and chutneys.*

Angelica fruit soufflé

Wash and dice the fruit into small pieces. Cook in juice or wine until softened, but do not allow to disintegrate.

Slice the angelica stems into small sections, then candy in melted honey over a low heat. Crush the seeds and peppercorns, using a pestle and mortar.

Pre-heat the oven to 300 °F (150 °C). Lightly beat the eggs and add the angelica and spices. Place the fruit in a buttered dish and pour the egg mixture over the top.

Bake for approx. 1 hour in a pre-heated oven until the egg mixture has set.

2 pears
2 apples
2 quinces
20 plums
Scant ½ cup (100 ml) juice or wine
handful of angelica stems
3½ tbsp (100 g) honey
½ tsp each of cumin seeds, anise seeds, fennel seeds, peppercorns
4 eggs
knob of butter

FENNEL a sweet herb to warm the stomach
(Foeniculum vulgare) Apiaceae

BRONZE FENNEL
(Foeniculum vulgare v. rubrum) Apiaceae

Bronze fennel may not be as robust as its green cousin, which has long tap roots to anchor itself deep in the ground and can grow in the same spot for years, maturing to majestic heights, but, as far as flavor is concerned, it actually seems to be superior. Be that as it may, its reddish-brown, feathery fronds make a delightful splash in the garden. The umbels of yellow flowers produced by both varieties are often buzzing with insects, especially hoverflies. We are already familiar with fennel, with its unmistakable aroma, as a vegetable variety and as a classic herbal tea for stomach remedies, or a drink for babies. I always associate fennel in my mind with being snuggled under a blanket in winter, cupping a steaming cup of fennel tea in my hands, letting the aroma of its warmth work its magic.

Spelt and herb fritters VEGAN

2 cups (250 g) organic spelt flakes
1 cup (250 ml) hot water
3 tbsp (25 g) each of sesame seeds,
sunflower seeds, linseed,
flaked almonds
2 tbsp (10 g) minced fennel leaves
approx. 1 tbsp (5 g), when chopped, each of
parsley, cilantro, shepherd's needle,
chervil, ground elder,
cow parsley, lovage, chives
3 tbsp (30 g), when minced, each of carrots,
parsnips, celery
salt, pepper, nutmeg
small amount of rapeseed or olive oil

Pour the hot water over the spelt flakes, seasoned with salt to taste, then leave to soak for at least an hour.

Wash, dry, then finely chop the vegetables and herbs, then mix the chopped ingredients with the spelt and seeds. Season again to taste. Leave to stand for a while, then season again, if necessary, before kneading all the ingredients together thoroughly.

Shape the mixture into patties. Heat a little oil in a skillet over a moderate heat and fry on both sides until golden brown.

Serve with a wild herb salad, or another of your choice.

CILANTRO love it or hate it
(Coriandrum sativum) Apiaceae

Cilantro tends to be used more prolifically in southern climes. This herb, which is one of my favorites, was also very popular with the ancient Greeks and Romans. Since I am constantly on the look-out for this distinctive aroma and for edible umbrel flowers, a friend of mine once brought me back a relative of cilantro from Puerto Rico. Cilantro and its cousin, culantro or Mexican coriander (*Eryngium foetidum*), also known as recao, both exude the same wonderful cilantro aroma. This same intense fragrance is also found in Vietnamese cilantro (*Polygonum odoratum*), a member of the knotweed family, as well as in vap ca, also known as the chameleon plant (*Houttuynia cordata*), both of which are easy to cultivate in our gardens.

Pork tenderloin coated in herbs and bacon Serves 4

Wash and drain the herbs, then tear off and finely chop the leaves. Pre-heat the oven to 350 °F (180 °C).

Arrange four portions of 4 strips of bacon side by side and overlapping. Sprinkle the herb mixture over the top to make a bed of herbs, leaving one side clear.

Season the tenderloin pieces with salt and pepper and place each one on top of the herbs. Roll them up firmly and tuck in the ends.

Sauté the pork on all sides in a hot skillet, starting with the side with the join. Then cook in the pre-heated oven for approx. 15 minutes.

Remove from the oven, allow to rest for a short while, then cut into slices diagonally. Serve with a dark gravy, potatoes mashed with butter, and green beans.

4 slices of lean pork tenderloin (5½ oz (150 g) each)
16 bacon strips
fresh herbs, e.g. dill, thyme, parsley, cilantro, rosemary
salt, pepper

A recipe by Sebastian Schuff

LOVAGE queen of soups
(Levisticum officinale) Apiaceae

Lovage seems to thrive like mad in some gardens, but where we live, it does not seem to want to grow in the quantities we would like. Although I manage to cultivate seedlings and baby plants to sell on, there does not seem to be any spot in our garden where it is happy, although it never disappears altogether and always manages to provide an adequate supply of seeds.

Commonly known as "Maggi herb" (because the plant's taste is reminiscent of Maggi soup seasoning), the plant was mainly cultivated for its seeds in Roman cuisine. However, lovage is not only an excellent seasoning in soup but is also good for intensifying flavor, if used sparingly. In this respect, it is compatible with virtually anything or, if you really like its flavor, it could be used to create dishes featuring lovage as the key ingredient or maybe added to a breadcrumb coating or topping. It would also be ideal for incorporating into a Thanksgiving meal.

PARSLEY favorite everyday herb
(Petroselinum crispum) Apiaceae

No herb is more commonplace and universal than good old parsley. And yet, I bet that most people would only give it a thought if it were suddenly no longer available at the supermarket or farmer's market. What would happen to the obligatory parsley garnish which decorates every plate in a good restaurant? We barely even think about parsley: it is just an integral part of the dish!

And why should this be so? It is, after all, such an accommodating herb. It thrives all year round in any location and just grows and grows and grows. It can even be cultivated throughout the winter on a windowsill. Virtually no other herb is as easy-going, although some gardeners do actually have problems with it, as I do with lovage.

It also goes with virtually any dish, does it not? Not only will this plant adapt to any environment, but it demonstrates the same degree of flexibility in the kitchen, intensifying the flavor of one dish, enhancing or mellowing that of another, without itself monopolizing the limelight.

Yet it could if it wanted to! Just try adding a really large amount of parsley to freshly boiled potatoes, served simply with butter. For any vegans among you, I recommend almond butter instead of dairy butter. In either case, the flavor of the parsley will really come into its own. We are the first to admit that it is simply unbeatable!

SHEPHERD'S NEEDLE OR VENUS' COMB
modest but elegant little herb
(Scandix pecten-veneris) Apiaceae

My winter-hardy shepherd's needle seemed to feel completely at home in my garden right from day one, and since then it has thrived, flowered, self-seeded, and spread to wherever it could find a spare patch of soil. I come across new seedlings several times a year and, because it is so small, it can easily tuck itself in anywhere. No sooner has it germinated than the entire plant—flowers, leaves, and stem—is ready to harvest. The delicate, feathery, dill-like leaves taste like a combination of carrot, caraway, celery, and parsley and can be used in the same way as the last. The flavor of the seeds is mainly reminiscent of caraway seeds.

Potato cakes with shepherd's needle

Boil the potatoes in their skins, peel them while still hot, then feed them through a grinder, along with the onion and shepherd's needle. Add the butter, knead lightly, then chill in the refrigerator.

Shape the potato mixture into little patties, then fry on both sides in ghee until golden brown.

3–4 medium (300 g) potatoes
1 onion, minced
1 handful of shepherd's needle
knob of butter
salt, pepper, nutmeg
ghee (clarified butter) for frying

TIP   *Since shepherd's needle does not seem to be restricted to any particular season or location, it is ideal for planting in tubs or window boxes. It is well worth allowing this plant with its modest disposition a place in the garden.*

Five-umbrel dip

Wash, dry, and finely chop the herbs. Blend the quark, cream cheese, and crème fraîche with the chopped herbs and mustard. Season to taste with salt and pepper. If the mixture is too thick, add a little cream or oil.

1 cup (250 g) quark
1 cup (250 g) cream cheese
gen. ¾ cup (200 g) crème fraîche
1 handful each of lovage, parsley, fennel, dill, chives, and bearwort (or chervil and/or cilantro instead)
salt, pepper, 1 tbsp mustard
small amount of cream or oil, if required

TIP   *Goes particularly well with tender young zucchini, cucumber, carrots, sticks of celery, or fennel bulb.*

Parsley pasta Serves 4

3 bunches of parsley
small amount of water
3½ cups (300 g) spelt flour
⅔ cup (100 g) durum wheat semolina,
or durum wheat flour (if you are not using
a pasta-making machine: small amount of
buckwheat flour)

TIP   *If desired, you can also use ⅔ cup
(150 ml) liquid including the parsley, topped
up instead with some oil and a pinch of salt.*

Roughly chop and purée the parsley to a very smooth paste, adding a little water, if required. The end product should amount to no more than a generous ¾ cup (200 ml) of liquid, including the parsley.

Combine the spelt flour and durum wheat semolina, then add the liquid parsley mixture and knead the ingredients into a smooth dough. If the dough is not soft enough, add a little water, a few drops at a time. If the dough is too sticky, sprinkle in a little more flour.

Feed the pasta dough through a pasta-making machine or else roll it out very thinly and cut it into narrow strips. I usually cut the dough in two, then roll each lump out very thinly using a rolling pin.

If the sheet of dough becomes too big to handle, you can sprinkle buckwheat flour over the pasta sheet, fold it up, and carefully roll it out again. Next, fold it over again, and sprinkle with buckwheat flour to prevent it sticking together. This leaves you with a roll of dough which you can then slice into thin strips of pasta.

Once you have finished preparing the pasta, it can be cooked, either fresh or dry, in just a few minutes in a large saucepan of boiling water.

Parasol mushrooms with parsley Serves 4

2 large or 8 small parasol mushrooms
½ bunch of parsley
½ a garlic clove
2 eggs
⅔ cup (100 g) flour
½ cup (70 g) freshly grated white
breadcrumbs
3 tbsp (30 g) freshly grated Parmesan
salt, pepper
fat, for frying

A recipe by Marta Meli-Czeburko

Cut off the mushroom stems and gently brush clean the heads, carefully removing any detritus from the gills.

Wash the parsley, pat dry, and finely chop. Finely chop the garlic clove likewise.

Lightly beat the eggs. Season the mushrooms with salt and pepper and dip first in flour, then in the beaten egg mixture.

Mix the breadcrumbs, Parmesan, parsley, and garlic together and coat the mushrooms in the mixture.

Fry the mushrooms in hot fat on both sides for 2–3 minutes until golden brown.

SWEET CICELY light as a feather and tasting of licorice

(Myrrhis odorata and Scandix odorata) Apiaceae

Native sweet cicely is totally winter-hardy, comes up every year, and is robust, undemanding, reliable, and, once settled in a garden, inde-structible. Its seeds germinate after a light frost and it is very easy to propagate. The leaves of sweet cicely are fern-like and very softly hairy. They have a sweet flavor, immediately reminiscent of anise or licorice. Its seeds, if eaten while still green and immature, have a strong flavor and are very popular with my seminar participants, provided one likes the taste of licorice.

The first leaves can be picked in early spring for sweetening and season-ing purposes. However, the fun really begins with the start of the rhubarb harvest as sweet cicely seems to just neutralize the furry acidic effect on the teeth caused by this giant sorrel. You can enjoy a delicious rhubarb cake without the furry-teeth feeling, but also without the taste of licorice. Sweet cicely and rhubarb combine to create a wonderful composition of their own—naturally delicious with a yeast dough base and topped with crumble!

Sweet cicely syrup Makes approx. 1 quart (1 liter)

Chop the leaves, stems, and fruits of sweet cicely, then boil in plenty of water for approx. 20 minutes.

Strain the sweet cicely, reserving the water. Then simmer the water and sugar together. Transfer the syrup to jars and close with a screw-top lid.

1 handful of sweet cicely
1 quart (1 l) water
gen. 1 cup (250 g) sugar

Rhubarb crisp with sweet cicely

Wash the rhubarb and cut into sections. Finely chop the sweet cicely, then sprinkle over the rhubarb along with the sugar. Leave to marinate until the rhubarb begins to release its juices. Drain well.

Pre-heat the oven to 300 °F (150 °C). Knead the flour, butter, and sugar together into a pastry mix. Press half the mixture into a spring-form pan, then cover with the drained chunks of rhubarb. Crumble the remaining pastry over the rhubarb, then bake in the pre-heated oven for approx. 1 hour until the edges are golden brown.

Sweet cicely will mellow the tartness of the rhubarb.

3 large sticks of rhubarb
scant ½ cup (100 g) sugar
5 stems of sweet cicely
5 cups (600 g) flour
3½ sticks (400 g) butter
scant 1 cup (200 g) sugar

ORACH & CO. leafy giants and other members of the amaranth family

RED ORACH

(Atriplex hortensis) Amaranthaceae

Were it not for red orach, my natural herb garden would probably not exist and my passion for plants would be all the poorer without this wonderful edible salad plant. Although orach grows all over the place and is completely undemanding, adequate room, nutrients, and water are needed to get the best from this plant over as long a period as possible. The growing season of this popular salad ingredient and spinach-type plant is much too short, which is why I always try and cultivate as much of it as possible. If orach is too densely packed together or too dry, it will quickly flower and its leaves will become tough. Its close relative, giant goosefoot, also known as giant tree-spinach (*Chenopodium giganteum*), grows somewhat longer and becomes considerably taller, and its leaves can be picked until well into the fall, even if the plant has already begun to seed. There is little difference in flavor between the two. The giant "Magenta Spreen," which can grow up to 12–13 feet (4 meters) high in the greenhouse, is possibly slightly nuttier in flavor and crunchier. Orach varieties, whether green, red, or purple, are simply deliciously tender and a little tart. They are well worth cultivating in the garden simply to provide color and structure. No salad could be easier to pick and prepare. The leaves are delicious and versatile and suitable for use as spinach, in quiches, lasagne, or soup. Beets (*Beta*), including mangolds, chard, beet, sugar beet, and fodder beet, types of amaranth, spinach (*Spinacia*), Good King Henry or poor man's asparagus, and strawberry spinach are also members of the amaranth family.

TIP
Red orach can also be used as a lovely red colorant for rice or pasta.

Cream of orach soup VEGAN

Peel and finely chop the onions, then sweat in a little oil in a saucepan.

Peel and slice the potatoes into wafer-thin slices. Then add to the onions and pour in the white wine, plus a dash of agave syrup and however much water you require. Bring to the boil and simmer until the potatoes are tender.

Add the orach and lovage, allow to simmer for a few minutes, then purée or press the ingredients through a sieve and season to taste with salt, pepper, and nutmeg.

2 onions
2 tbsp oil
3 potatoes
gen. ¾ cup (200 ml) white wine
agave syrup
water, as required (depending on what consistency is desired)
6 handfuls of red and/or green orach
fresh lovage
salt, pepper
grated nutmeg, to taste

STRAWBERRY SPINACH an original treat for the
taste buds *(Chenopodium foliosum), (Chenopodium capitatum) Chenopodioideae*

These two varieties of strawberry sticks not only increase diversity in the garden but also constitute a welcome addition to the menu and will delight your taste buds! It is quite simply a joy to get to know over the course of the years so many different types of plants, which can be turned into salads and spinach-type dishes. Although these two are easy to cultivate, they do need rich, constantly damp soil in order to produce a plentiful supply of leaves and to discourage them from flowering too early. The bright red strawberry-like clusters of fruit also contain the seeds, which self-seed very easily. As a result, your garden will never again be without strawberry sticks.

The jagged, heart-shaped leaves may not look much at first glance, but their delicate, unusual flavor makes them something very special. They are slightly nutty, creamy, and very distinctive in a delicate way: I would not like to be without this culinary delight. I eat most of the leaves raw as a salad ingredient—but the name itself suggests how it can be used in the kitchen. It tastes good on its own as a spinach dish or mixed with orach or stinging nettles. The pretty berry-filled vines also make delightful table decorations, and the sweetish berries can be used as a garnish for salads or be whisked into a frothy topping for strawberry spinach soup.

Ré's 6 × 6 fritters **VEGAN**

approx. 2 cups vegetable stock
6 kernels: approx. 100 g (altogether)
almonds, walnuts, sesame seeds, sunflower seeds, pistachios, pine nuts, ground or chopped
6 herbs: approx. 1½ cups (altogether)
parsley, leeks, lovage, hyssop, marjoram, chervil
6 spices: salt, pepper, nutmeg, mustard, paprika powder, turmeric
6 vegetables: approx. 1 cup (altogether)
carrots, leeks, kohrabi, parsnips, zucchini, pumpkin, very finely chopped

Pour the vegetable stock over the kernels, leave to soak for a while, then add the other ingredients.

Knead all the ingredients together, leave to stand for a while, then season to taste. If the mixture is too wet, add a little spelt flour. If it is too dry, add a little water or stock.

Shape the mixture into patties, then fry in a skillet for 6 minutes on each side.

TIP *These hearty fritters make a wonderful accompaniment to the mild yet distinctive flavor of strawberry spinach.*

TARRAGON bittersweet aromatic miracle

(Artemisia dracunculus) Asteraceae

Tarragon, a robust and undemanding plant, the most aromatic variety of which is French tarragon, is extremely unassuming in the garden or in tubs and virtually indestructible. Only my ground elder has managed to force my tarragon stocks into retreat. The better-known artemisia plants used for culinary or herbal remedy purposes include southern worm-wood (*Artemisia abrotanum*), absinthe or wormwood (*Artemisia absin-thium*), mugwort (*Artemisia vulgaris*) and annual mugwort (*Artemisia annua*).

I eat the first, fleshy shoots, a springtime rival for ground elder, on my bread at breakfast, or they can be made into a spread. It is always an inexpressible delight, following a winter deprived of herbs, to enjoy the first new shoots of fresh green. From this point on, tarragon grows tire-lessly into the fall. The more you harvest, the more the plant will bush out. The plant's delightfully scented leaves can continue to be harvested well beyond the flowering season, and these delicate but intensely aro-matic leaves are ideal for freezing or drying. Either way, the aroma of French tarragon remains perfectly preserved.

TIP   *Wormwood plants make good neighbors for currant bushes.*

Tarragon eggs

It is best to boil a few more eggs than you need since some eggs cannot always be peeled or sliced cleanly. Hard-boiled eggs should be chilled in the refrigerator for a while before use.

Peel the eggs and cut in half lengthways. Carefully scoop out the egg yolk, then pass through a sieve.

Combine the egg yolks with the rest of the ingredients and, if necessary, color with a little turmeric or saffron. Add the finely chopped tarragon leaves.

Transfer the egg-yolk cream to a piping bag, then pipe into the halved eggs. Garnish with tarragon tips or flowers.

4 hard-boiled eggs
4 tsp crème fraîche
1 tsp mustard
salt, pepper, nutmeg
saffron or turmeric for coloring, if the eggs
are too pale
tarragon leaves and tips or flowers

"Come again tomorrow" stuffed pancakes

For the pancakes
1 cup (250 ml) milk
⅔ cup (100 g) flour
2 eggs
salt
oil, for frying

For the filling
1 cup (250 g) cream cheese
gen. ½ cup (150 g) sour cream
pepper, salt
1 handful tarragon
1 bunch each of lovage, chives, parsley, oregano

Mix the pancake ingredients into a smooth batter. Using a small skillet, cook a batch of thin pancakes over a moderate heat, without turning!

Wash, dry, and finely chop the herbs. To make the filling, combine the cream cheese, sour cream, spices, and herbs.

Spoon a teaspoon of filling onto the cooked side of each pancake, then fold the pancake in half and fold the corners into the middle to make a square parcel. Fry the parcel in the skillet on both sides until golden brown.

For a sweeter version, use sugar or maple syrup instead of salt and pepper, or, if you prefer to use herbs, sweet cicely or angelica would be ideal.

TIP *"Come again tomorrow" is actually a Baltic recipe from the homeland of my father Richard, although the filling there is made with ground meat, that is to say leftovers—so that might mean "Come back tomorrow, and there'll be something different." However, our "Come again tomorrow" pancakes are so delicious that you can just keep on eating them!*

GOOD KING HENRY steadfast garden companion
(Chenopodium bonus-henricus)

It was Katharina's culinary experiments with Good King Henry which first made me aware of this herb's robustness and other qualities. Being an ambitious cultivator of organically grown herbs and with my deep passion for diversity and for preserving species, I have, naturally enough, often over-extended myself. It is disappointing enough when herbs sometimes simply do not thrive, but it is even more disheartening to see them keep disappearing. However, Good King Henry, which I thoroughly disliked in its raw state and which I never really liked, even cooked like spinach, because of its bitter juices, has turned out to be one of the most tenacious plants of all. Once planted, it has thrived full of gratitude in its allotted spot, producing an abundance of green growth and spreading on its own by self-seeding. As a sort of tribute to the steely loyalty it has shown me and the human race since the Stone Age, I decided to ask Katharina to devise a dish to incorporate its lush foliage, and guess what! The result was a wonderful recipe for ravioli stuffed with ricotta and Good King Henry.

Good King Henry ravioli

To make the sauce, finely dice the shallots. Chop the carrot, leek, and tomatoes. Strip the leaves off the lemon thyme sprigs.

Sweat the shallots in a little olive oil, then add the leek, carrot, tomatoes, agave syrup, tomato paste, pepper, and salt and continue to cook. Pour in the white wine and add a scant ½ cup (100 ml) water. Simmer until the liquid has reduced by half.

Add the cream and lemon thyme leaves. Cook until the mixture has once again reduced by half.

Pass the sauce through a fine sieve and thoroughly press the juices from the vegetables. If necessary, thicken the sauce with a little cornstarch before seasoning with salt and pepper to taste.

To make the filling, peel and chop the shallots and garlic. Tear off the sweet yarrow leaves and finely chop. Roughly chop the Good King Henry leaves.

Fry the shallots in olive oil until translucent, then add the Good King Henry, garlic, and sweet yarrow, and cook until softened and the Good King Henry leaves begin to disintegrate. Season with salt and pepper. Remove the skillet from the heat, stir in the ricotta, then season the mixture to taste and set aside.

To make the ravioli, combine the two types of flour, add the water, and knead the mixture into a smooth dough. Divide into portions, then, on a floured work surface, roll out two portions at a time into sheets, each approx. ⅛ inch (2 mm) thick. Spoon walnut-sized portions of the filling onto one sheet of pasta spaced at intervals of about 2 inches (5 cm) apart.

Beat the egg yolk with a fork. Brush egg yolk around the edges of the pasta sheet to make them stick firmly together. Then, placing the second sheet of pasta on top of the first, work over the pasta, using your fingers to press the sheets together around the filling. Cut into squares of ravioli and press around the edges with a fork. Repeat this process with the remaining portions of pasta dough. Cook the ravioli in plenty of salted water for approx. 5–7 minutes. Drain and add a little butter.

To make the pesto, purée the leaves in a tall container. Gradually add the remaining ingredients, except for the Parmesan. Finish by stirring in the Parmesan and seasoning to taste.

Serve the ravioli with the creamy tomato sauce and grate the Parmesan over the top. Serve with an accompaniment of the lemon pesto.

For the sauce

3 shallots
1 carrot
½ leek
6 tomatoes
4 sprigs of lemon thyme
2 tbsp olive oil
1 tbsp agave syrup
1 tbsp tomato paste
⅔ cup (150 ml) white wine
⅔ cup (100 g) heavy cream
cornstarch, salt, pepper
5 oz piece (150 g) Parmesan cheese, for serving

For the filling

2 shallots
1 garlic clove
3 sprigs of sweet yarrow
14 oz (400 g) young leaves (stems removed) of Good King Henry
2 tbsp olive oil
1 cup (250 g) ricotta
salt, pepper

For the pasta dough

2½ cups (300 g) spelt flour
⅔ cup (100 g) durum wheat semolina, or durum wheat flour
¾ cup (200 ml) water
1 egg yolk

For the pesto

1¼ well-packed cups (75 g) basil
2 tbsp pine nuts
leaves from 5 stems each of lemon thyme and lemon savory
¾ cup (200 ml) good-quality olive oil
½ tsp salt
pepper
2 tbsp freshly grated Parmesan

A recipe by Katharina Schnabl

The gentle aromas of the south:

summer herbs

Many typical summer herbs belong to the labiate family, such as basil, savory, marjoram, rosemary, sage, thyme, oregano, mint, verbena, and hyssop, as well as dead nettles and sweet nettles, which have played an important culinary role in the kitchen for over 2,000 years and still continue to be a classic home remedy for colds or digestive problems.

However, the Romans, in particular, were used to a much broader range of spices and herbs, which we are only now beginning to discover. Naturally, people like Charles the Great and Hildegard von Bingen have also played a role in keeping these herbs alive and making sure we keep trying them out. My herb seminars, however, always give me the impression that some dramatic upheaval must have occurred, after which the use of herbs ceased to be a perfectly natural part of everyday life, turning instead into something that was verging on dangerous. My guess is that it had to do with the Inquisition and world wars, after which wild herbs were branded as diabolical or at best cheap and nasty. It is important to discover what sparked such deep-seated fear and dramatic change and try to overcome it, but I believe that the close relationship we have with herbs ultimately runs much deeper and is consequently all the more solid and there is no better way of demonstrating this than by eating the herbs themselves.

BASIL balsamic pepper
(Ocimum basilicum) Lamiaceae

Sadly, the growing period of basil is all too short to satisfy the constant demand for this sumptuous herb, at least if you want to cultivate it yourself in the garden or on a windowsill. Obviously, we can indulge our passion for basil anytime, summer or winter, simply by buying this delicious plant in organic food shops or a supermarket. It is remarkable how basil refuses to relinquish its strong aroma. I find many of the growing herbs sold in supermarkets very disappointing even though I myself have to rely on them sometimes during winters in Wuppertal.

A particular combination of ingredients often goes hand in hand with a planting partnership. It comes as no surprise, for example, that basil grows very happily at the base of tomato plants! Tomatoes also like parsley as a companion plant, and what would tabbouleh be without parsley?

TIP *If you plan to plant basil in pots, I suggest planting it in good soil, possibly compost, in a large pot right from the start. Always cut off whole stems to encourage further growth. Just plucking the leaves weakens the plant too much and it will not last long. Basil needs plenty of light and good soil. Avoid waterlogged or extremely dry locations.*

Maiga's tabbouleh with millet **VEGAN**

¾ cup (150 g) millet
1 lb (500 g) tomatoes
1 large red onion
olive oil
1 lemon
3 bunches parsley
1 bunch cilantro
1 sprig peppermint
1 sprig Japanese water pepper
or pinch of chili powder
salt, pepper

Cook the millet until soft with a pinch of salt, then leave to cool. Meanwhile, finely dice the tomatoes.

Finely dice the onion, then mix with olive oil, lemon juice, finely chopped parsley, and cilantro, and leave to marinate. Add the tomatoes and season with salt and pepper to taste.

When cool, add the millet to the tomato mix and season with finely chopped mint and Japanese water pepper leaves.

TIP *Basil can also be used instead of cilantro. The photo shows Good King Henry ravioli made from parsley pasta as described on page 52.*

WINTER SAVORY
(Satureja montana) Lamiaceae

This robust perennial is a hardy evergreen and, like its annual cousin, summer savory (*Satureja hortensis*), is particularly happy growing among beans and other pulses.

Its peppery flavor is traditionally used to season not only any bean-based dishes but also soups and other hearty foods. The addition of winter savory to these dishes not only has the obvious benefit of extra flavor but also helps to alleviate the effects of flatulence caused by pulses, making them more digestible.

Potato pancakes VEGAN

2¼ lbs (1 kg) potatoes
2 carrots
1 onion
2–3 tbsp spelt flour, for thickening
1 handful of herbs, e.g. bearwort (in spring), chives, field garlic, garlic chives, parsley, lovage, common hogweed,
dill, fennel, yarrow
oil, for frying
salt, pepper

Wash, peel, and grate the potatoes and carrots. Grate or finely chop the onion, then mix with the potatoes.

Depending on how much liquid has accumulated from the above, stir in the flour and season. Alternatively, you can squeeze the potatoes firmly in a kitchen towel to remove excess liquid.

Wash and pick over the herbs, dry, then finely chop and add to the potato mixture.

Heat the oil in a skillet, then shape the potatoes into thin patties and fry on both sides until golden brown.

Strawberry and lavender punch with Aztec sweet herb

½ lb (250 g) fresh strawberries
5 stems Aztec sweet herb
1 bottle dry sparkling wine or Prosecco
6–10 lavender flowers
punchbowl

A recipe by Marta Meli-Czeburko

Clean the strawberries, then cut into bite-sized pieces. Tear the leaves off the sweet herb, then place in a punchbowl.

Pour in the sparkling wine or Prosecco and chill for at least 2½ hours.

Before serving, add 1 or 2 lavender flowers to each glass.

LEMON SAVORY

(Satureja montana var. Citriodora) Lamiaceae

The lemon version of winter savory, which can grow into majestic plants both in the garden and on the balcony, is very similar in growth and habit to the original.
Its very peppery taste is accompanied by a strong lemon aroma, making the herb particularly suitable for dishes such as Swabian-style cheese *Spätzle*, for example.

TIP   *Woody herbs such as savory, lavender, rosemary, or hyssop can be cultivated into hedges or edging around vegetable gardens. It is best to cut the herbs back in August to give them time to produce more growth. Cutting back too late may cause problems if there is an early frost.*

MARJORAM

(Origanum majorana) Lamiaceae

My favorite type of oregano is marjoram, the aroma of which is familiar to us as a classic seasoning for meat dishes. Although it is actually very simple to cultivate, either as an annual or as a biennial, I always seem to forget that these plants begin to flower very early, after which they no longer produce many green leaves. I wish I could go on using it for longer, considering all the potato dishes and bread toppings it can be used for. In order to be able to maximize the amount of marjoram harvested, it would have to be sown afresh every few weeks, in the same way as lettuce, cilantro, or dill.

LAVENDER

(Lavandula angustifolia) Lamiaceae

Although lavender is regarded as a traditional companion to roses, I have noticed that it does not like to be demoted to the status of a mere companion plant. Whereas roses need well-composted soil, lavender prefers a more barren habitat. We should, therefore, give lavender its own leading role or else plant it as a fragrant border hedge instead of the familiar beech hedging.
In culinary terms, lavender can be used to enhance all kinds of flavors, ranging from sweet to savory. I have flavored chocolates and jams with lavender leaves or unopened flower buds and find that it goes extremely well with game dishes as an ingredient in a creamy game sauce.

OREGANO
(Origanum vulgare) Lamiaceae

Oregano, like lavender and sage, comes in many different colors, aromas, and shapes. Golden oregano or delicately scented and silvery-leaved varieties are just as robust as compact oregano, a dwarf variety with a very mild but intensely fruity aroma. The spicy leaves of its Cretan cousin, on the other hand, are reminiscent of pepper and taste wonderful on pizzas or foccacia, though its tiny white flowers are unprepossessing in comparison to native oregano, which grows all over the countryside full of pink flowers in late summer and cannot fail to attract attention thanks to the multitude of buzzing insects surrounding it. Traditionally, oregano is a main ingredient on Italian pizza, and in the natural herb garden, no herbal tea is complete without aromatic oregano flowers.

Chestnut and venison tartlets
Makes approx. 40 tartlets

Make the short pastry by kneading together the flour, salt, egg, butter, and vinegar. Chill in the refrigerator.

For the filling, wash the herbs, pat dry, and finely chop. Finely chop the onions and slice the leek. Season the venison with salt and pepper then mix in the chopped herbs, onions, egg, or cream.

Boil the chestnuts in a little water until soft, then drain, purée, and season with salt, pepper, and nutmeg. Add just enough crème fraîche to keep the mixture firm but still soft enough to be piped through a piping bag.

Pre-heat the oven to 300 °F (150 °C). Roll out the pastry, cut out circles, and line small tartlet molds so that the pastry edge comes up to the top edge of the mold.

Place one spoonful of meat mixture into the center and pipe chestnut purée around the edge. Bake the tartlets in the pre-heated oven for approx. 30 minutes.

For the short pastry cases
1⅔ cups (200 g) spelt flour
salt
1 egg
⅓ cup (80 g) butter
1 tbsp vinegar

For the herb and meat filling
1¾ cups (400 g) ground venison
3 onions
1 small leek
2 sprigs each of oregano, rosemary, hyssop
5 sprigs thyme
3 sprigs marjoram
salt, pepper
1 egg, or ¾ cup (200 g) heavy cream

For the chestnut purée
approx. 40 (400 g) chestnuts, shells removed
1 cup (¼ l) stock
salt, pepper, nutmeg
1 cup (250 g) crème fraîche

ROSEMARY

(Rosmarinus officinalis) Lamiaceae

If you live in the Hunsrück region, you will be delighted if you can manage to keep a rosemary plant alive over winter. But if you could see entire slopes covered in rosemary in the mountains of Andalusia, you would be completely lost for words. Rosemary grows there into giant bushes, sometimes flowering away in the middle of January, smelling beautiful in the midday sun next to thyme and common rue.

Latin literature often includes many mentions of these typical Mediterranean herbs. The labiates, especially, with their aromatic oils, can be used in all kinds of dishes. Who has not, for example, heard of rosemary potatoes?

Warning: *Pregnant women should not consume rue because this plant can have an abortifacient effect. Picking rue can also cause skin inflammation for those with sensitive skin.*

Rosemary brownies

For the brownies
5 oz (150 g) dark chocolate
4 tbsp (60g) sugar
2–3 sprigs rosemary
5 eggs
vanilla extract, to taste
1¾ sticks (200 g) butter
gen. 1⅓ cups (200 g) flour
6 tbsp (40 g) cocoa powder
5 oz (150 g) white chocolate

For the chocolate ganache
gen. ½ cup (150 g) heavy cream
5 oz (150 g) dark chocolate
2 tbsp (30 g) sugar

For the common rue ice cream
½ vanilla bean
1 cup (¼ l) milk
gen. 1 cup (250 g) heavy cream
scant ½ cup (100 g) sugar
5 stalks of common rue
5–6 (100 g) egg yolks

A recipe by Michael Daus

To make the ice cream, slit the vanilla bean lengthways and scrape out the seed pulp. Bring the milk, cream, sugar, vanilla pulp, and empty bean to the boil. Add the rue and steep for 20 minutes, then strain the liquid through a sieve. Blend the reserved liquid, a little at a time, with the egg yolks. Heat the egg mixture in a bain-marie until it takes on a creamy consistency (approx. 180 °F/82 °C). Stir until cool, then freeze.

To make the ganache, heat the cream and sugar together until just bubbling. Melt the chocolate and the butter in the bain-marie, then pour the cream mixture onto the dark chocolate, stir the ingredients into a smooth paste, and leave to chill for at least 2 hours in the refrigerator.

Pre-heat the oven to 320 °F (160 °C). To make the brownie topping, melt the chocolate and sugar in the bain-marie. Strip off and finely chop the rosemary needles, add to the chocolate, and leave to infuse the flavor.

Whisk the eggs, sugar, and vanilla extract into a pale, frothy consistency using an electric hand blender, then slowly stir in the melted chocolate mixture. Sift the flour and slowly mix with the cocoa powder. Gradually stir into the mixture.
Finally, chop the white chocolate and stir the chunks into the mixture. Transfer into brownie molds and bake for about 15 minutes in the preheated oven. Once it has cooled, whisk the ganache using the hand blender. Serve the brownies with the ganache and ice cream.

CREEPING THYME

(Thymus serphyllum) Lamiaceae

Not all herbs come from southern climes. Creeping thyme and oregano are herbs native to Europe. Fast-growing, creeping thyme spreads into delightful carpets in the garden or in window boxes and does not mind being picked by the handful. Thanks to Hildegard von Bingen, this little herb has become more familiar again.

Creeping thyme looks lovely spilling out over the edges of pots or balcony boxes and grows happily alongside other plants, providing shade for their roots.

Ré's chestnut cake

Knead together all the ingredients for the base, then wrap in foil and chill.

Pre-heat the oven to 300 °F (150 °C). Line a spring-form pan with the pastry base, leaving a raised edge around the outside. Pre-bake for approx. 15 minutes.

For the filling, boil the chestnuts in a small amount of water until soft, purée, then leave to cool. Whisk the cream until stiff, then fold in the sugar.

Stir in the chestnut purée, cornstarch, and herbs and transfer the mixture onto the pastry base. Bake the cake at 300 °F (150 °C) for approx. 1 hour until the filling is firm (carry out a skewer test. Leave to cool.

Meanwhile, dust the work surface with confectioners' sugar and roll out the marzipan into a thin sheet, turning several times. Place on top of the cooled chestnut cake and press down gently.

Melt the chocolate topping in a bain-marie. Decorate the cake with a layer of chocolate and chocolate cookies.

For the base
1¾ cups (250 g) flour
1 tsp baking powder
⅔ cup (150 g) butter
1 egg
3½ tbsp (50 g) sugar

For the filling
gen. 1 lb (500 g) chestnuts, shelled
gen. 2 cups (500 g) heavy cream
⅓ cup (75 g) sugar
5½ tbsp (50 g) cornstarch
1 tsp fresh thyme leaves
2 tbsp confectioners' sugar
8 oz (250 g) block of marzipan
8 oz (250 g) chocolate, for coating
chocolate cookies, to decorate

SAGE
(Salvia officinalis) Lamiaceae

Sage is a herb which varies greatly in shape, fragrance, and flower or leaf color. Unfortunately, not all varieties are winter hardy and therefore need special over-wintering places. For me personally, in the Hunsrück, this is sadly not very practical, but there are nevertheless a few good varieties which have naturalized in our herb garden. One of these is the so-called lavender sage, whose leaves exude a hint of lavender in addition to the typical sage aroma, and another is a very beautiful variety with red leaves.

Sage is quite similar to lavender in terms of being suitable for sweet as well as savory dishes, and as well as enjoying classic sage butter pasta, I also love its flavor in chokeberry crumble.

When sage is in bloom, it looks remarkably like lavender—and the scent is equally intoxicating.

Chokeberry crisp with sage and Spanish thyme

Yeast dough, see page 125

approx. 2 handfuls of chokeberries
few leaves of sage or thyme

For the crisp
2 ⅔ cups (300 g) spelt flour
7 tbsp (100 g) butter
7 tbsp (100 g) almond butter or ordinary butter
scant ½ cup (100 g) sugar
salt

Make some yeast dough, according to the recipe, and line the base of a baking pan.

Pre-heat the oven to 300 °F (150 °C). Cover the yeast dough base with chokeberries, a little sugar, and chopped sage or thyme leaves.

Roughly knead the crisp ingredients together and crumble the ingredients over the chokeberries. Bake for half an hour in the pre-heated oven until the base and crisp topping turn golden brown.

THYME

(Thymus vulgaris) Lamiaceae

This herb, a favorite in Ancient Roman kitchens, is as familiar to us as basil, rosemary, or sage and is an integral part of any kitchen or household. Thyme will not survive the cold Hunsrück winters without protection, but it has flourished in the greenhouse into a majestic, woody shrub. As with oregano and sage, there are many different types of thyme, all with varying leaf colors and aromas. A lemon version of thyme with a wonderful aroma can sometimes be found on barren slopes which have been grazed by goats, for example. Lemon thyme (*Thymus vulgaris citriodorus*) and orange thyme (*Thymus fragrantissimus*) are available from all good garden centers.

SPANISH THYME

(Thymus zygis) Lamiaceae

My favorite variety meanwhile is now gray-leaved Spanish thyme. This undemanding plant can be easily cultivated on a balcony and be picked frequently. However, it must be protected from damp and cold. Although Spanish thyme resembles ordinary thyme, its unexpected aroma will surprise you. Its balsamic sweet fragrance also has fruity, orange overtones, followed by mandarin and vanilla, until eventually you get to something reminiscent of thyme.

Panna cotta with Spanish thyme, blackcurrants, and pink pepper

Place the milk and cream in a saucepan, add the gelatin substitute, sugar, and Spanish thyme, then bring to the boil and simmer over a low heat for approx. 15 minutes, stirring occasionally.

Remove the thyme from the pan, then transfer the mixture to molds and chill in the refrigerator for at least 4 hours.

Purée half the berries, then crush the pink peppercorns using a pestle and mortar. Mix the berry purée and crushed peppercorns together.

Serve the panna cotta with whole berries and fruit purée.

2½ cups (600 g) heavy cream
gen. ¾ cup (200 ml) milk
approx. 15 sprigs of Spanish thyme
2 tbsp sugar
1 sachet of agar agar (vegetarian gelatin substitute also known as kanten, available in Asian markets and health food stores)
8–9 oz (250 g) blackcurrants
1 tsp whole pink peppercorns

A recipe by Katharina Schnabel

Pan-cooked apple tart with caramelized cashew nuts and Spanish thyme

For the yeast dough

3 cups (350 g) spelt flour (type 630)
1 tsp dry yeast
1 cup (¼ l) warm water
1 tbsp sugar
2 tbsp soft butter
1 tsp salt

For the filling

leaves from a few sprigs of Spanish thyme
1¾ cups (200 g) cashew nuts
1 tbsp butter + extra for greasing
3 tbsp sugar
2–3 apples
ovenproof cast-iron skillet (9 inch/24 cm)

A recipe by Katharina Schnabel

To make the yeast dough, place half the water, the yeast, 1 tablespoon of sugar, and 1 tablespoon of flour in a large bowl (non-metal) and mix with a wooden or plastic spoon. Cover the mixture and leave to rest in a warm place for approx. 15–30 minutes until bubbles begin to form.

Add the remaining water and flour, together with the salt and soft butter, then knead the ingredients into a smooth dough. Pre-heat the oven to 390 °F (200 °C).

Grease the cast-iron skillet thoroughly with butter. Place the dough in the pan and spread it out, pulling up the rim to make a raised edge.

Melt the 1 tablespoon of butter in a skillet and heat over a moderate heat. Add the cashew nuts and the sugar, then cook until caramelized, turning the nuts frequently until they are coated in melted sugar. Place the caramelized nuts on a baking sheet and leave to cool.

Peel and slice the apples. Arrange them, slightly overlapping, on the dough base. Dot a little butter onto the apples, then sprinkle the cashew nuts evenly over the apples. Finish with sprinkling over thyme leaves, reserving a couple of sprigs for decoration.

Place the skillet in the pre-heated oven and bake for about 20 minutes until the dough is lightly browned.

Leave the pan-cooked apple tart to cool for a while, then sprinkle with the remaining thyme leaves. Cut the cake into slices and serve.

Hearty cheesecake   Serves 4

Mix the butter and flour together and stir in the salt and thyme to form a crumbly mixture. Stir in 1 to 2 tablespoons of ice-cold water, then spread the mixture evenly over the base of a springform pan measuring about 10 inches (26 cm) in diameter. Press down firmly, then chill in the fridge for about 1 hour.

Pre-heat the oven to 390 °F (200 °C). Pierce the base several times with a fork, cover with baking parchment and weight with a layer of dried beans or pie weights. Bake blind for approx. 15 minutes in the pre-heated oven, then remove and set aside to cool for a little while.

Meanwhile, prepare the filling: grate the goat's milk gouda, then mix with the lemon zest, soft chèvre, quark, olive oil and rosemary, blending well. Beat the eggs, then stir into the mixture. Season with salt and pepper. Spread the mixture over the pre-baked base.

Bake the cake in a fan oven pre-heated to 300 °F (150 °C). Remove from the oven and leave to cool completely, then carefully release it from the springform pan. Pluck the leaves off the herbs and sprinkle over the cheesecake. A green salad or fruity tomato salad make excellent accompaniments to this dish.

For the short pastry
gen. 1 cup (150 g) flour
pinch of fleur de sel
1 tbsp thyme
1/3 cup (75 g) butter
dried beans or pie weights, for baking blind

For the filling
gen. ¾ cup (100 g) goat's milk gouda
zest of 1 lemon
2 x 8 oz tubs (500 g) soft chèvre (goat's cheese)
2 x 8 oz tubs (500 g) quark (40 % fat)
2 tbsp olive oil
1 tbsp rosemary
2 eggs
salt, pepper

For the garnish
fresh herbs, e.g. cress, nasturtium leaves, basil

Cream tea Serves 4

To make the scones, combine the flour, baking powder, and butter, then blend in the food mixer.

Add the sugar and a pinch of salt, blend in the egg, and stir in the cream, a little at a time.

Pre-heat the oven to 355 °F (180 °C). Add the chopped chocolate to the mixture and shape into individual scones. Bake in the oven for approx. 10–12 minutes.

To make the drinking chocolate, bring the milk and cream to a boil. Stir in the chocolate a little at a time.

Add the herbs to the hot chocolate drink a few at a time and leave to steep for 5–6 minutes. Strain the drink into cups and serve with the scones.

For the scones
2 cups (280 g) flour
1 tbsp (10–12 g) baking powder
¾ stick (76 g) chilled butter, cubed
3½ tbsp (50 g) sugar
salt
1 egg
½ cup (120 g) light cream
3½ oz (100 g) dark chocolate, chopped

For the drinking chocolate
1¼ cups (300 g) light cream
gen. ¾ cup (200 ml) milk
5 oz (150 g) white chocolate
½ bunch sweet cicely
3 sprigs thyme

A recipe by Michael Daus

TIP *Chill the prepared scones in the refrigerator for approx. 2 hours so that the chocolate does not melt and run during baking.*

MINTS welcome face amid the diversity

My early attempts at gardening naturally had to include mints, which were fairly simple to propagate and relatively undemanding. And because mint grows well alongside potatoes, I went on to plant my first potatoes one day in a part of the garden which still contained mints planted by the previous owners. The resulting crop of potatoes was assuredly the most delicious I have ever harvested. I now no longer know precisely where so many colorful old varieties came from before the advent of the Internet. The handful of seed suppliers and other growers willing to exchange plants obviously supplied what I needed and nothing stood in the way of my passion for blue, red, and yellow potatoes. Since I am always on the look-out for interesting, tasty, practical varieties, I have also brought home lots of plants from my travels.

The tastiest variety to suit Hunsrück soil was a potato variety called "King Edward" from England. However, since I always intended at some point to earn money from my herbs, the vegetables all had to give way eventually, leaving the mints growing between all the wild herbs which germinate every year in the garden. But even the old, original mint eventually surrendered to other delicious herbs and has now sadly completely disappeared during the course of my many projects for redesigning the garden.

From a mixture of numerous varieties, aromas, tastes, and shapes, a handful of mints have emerged as the solid core for my natural herb garden which I can wholeheartedly recommend as plants that will not end up dominating the garden. Apple mint (*Mentha rotundifolia* or *Mentha suaveolens*) and ginger mint will quickly take over the entire garden with their invasive rooting habit. Only ground elder has managed to keep them in check.

If you grow mint in pots, you can obviously choose any kind you like, but you will need to maintain a plentiful supply of compost. One of the mints which we retained, for example, was the mild pineapple mint (*Mentha suaveolens "variegata"*), with its delightful, delicate, variegated leaves and extremely fruity aroma. Bergamot mint (*Mentha piperita var. citrata*) with its red-edged, circular leaves and distinct aroma of Earl Grey tea has become a common ingredient of delicious tea, and strawberry mint (*Mentha species*) is frequently added to the sponge mixture when we make strawberry or raspberry cream swiss roll. This variety of mint smells like strawberry cream candy and makes a sweet little garden or pot plant with its delicate, crinkly little leaves and tiny pink flowers.

From top to bottom: catmint, Corsican mint, pineapple mint

Swiss roll with strawberries and strawberry mint

To make the cake, separate the eggs. Whisk the whites until stiff with some of the sugar and a pinch of salt.

Whisk the yolks with the rest of the sugar until the mixture turns pale. Stir in the liquid, then sift in the flour.

Carefully fold in the egg whites. Finely chop the strawberry mint or other herbs before mixing them into the cake mixture. This will give the cake a stronger herb aroma.

Pre-heat the oven to 340 °F (170 °C). Line a shallow rectangular baking pan with an edge with baking parchment. Pour in the batter and level. Bake immediately in the pre-heated oven for approx. 25 minutes until the surface turns golden brown.

Flip upside down onto a kitchen towel while still warm and peel off the baking parchment. Roll up the sponge layer, then leave to cool.

Whisk the cream and cream stabilizer together, then stir in the sugar and berries. Carefully unroll the sponge when cool and spread the cream mixture over the surface.

Roll up the sponge once more and chill in the refrigerator. Sprinkle with confectioners' sugar just before serving.

For the sponge
5 large eggs
scant 1 cup (200 g) sugar
small amount of liquid
(milk, water, rose water, juice,
depending on subsequent flavor)
gen. 1⅓ cups (200 g) flour
salt

For the filling
2 cups + 2 tbsp (500 g) heavy cream
1–2 sachets of whipped cream stabilizer
3–4 tbsp (50 g) sugar (depending on how tart the berries are)
fresh strawberries or raspberries, depending on season
bunch of strawberry mint or Japanese water pepper, as a
contrast to the sweet berries
confectioners' sugar, for dusting

Hot tea for cold days   Makes approx. 1 quart (1 liter)

Place all the herbs in a teapot. Add boiling water and leave to steep for 5–8 minutes.

Warning: *Use borage only in small quantities, as if consumed in excess it can cause liver dysfunction. Occasional consumption is considered safe.*

2 umbrels of elderberry blossom
3 leaves broadleaf plantain
1 tsp lime blossoms
1 sprig thyme
1 sprig sage
5 mallow flowers
5 rosehips
3 raspberry leaves
3 borage leaves
1 sprig mint

A recipe by Marta Meli-Czeburko

Mitzi's grapefruit lemonade with lemon verbena

For the syrup

2 lemons
2 limes
1 grapefruit
1 orange
5 sprigs mint
3 umbrels of elderberry blossoms
1 quart (1 l) water
4½ cups (1 kg) sugar

To make 1 quart (1 liter) lemonade

ice cubes
5 slices of lime
5 slices of orange
5 slices of grapefruit
1 bunch of lemon verbena
1 quart (1 l) still mineral water

A recipe by Marta Meli-Czeburko

To make the syrup, wash all the citrus fruits, elderberry flowers, and mint, then chop finely. Crush gently, place in a saucepan with 1 quart (1 liter) of water, and leave overnight.

The following day, filter the herb water through a strainer into a large saucepan and add the sugar. Boil until the liquid turns syrupy. Transfer while still hot into prepared bottles and leave to cool.

To make the lemonade, add the slices of citrus fruit to a carafe. Tear off the lemon verbena leaves and add to the carafe along with the ice cubes.

Pour in one part grapefruit syrup to seven parts mineral water and stir well.

Decorate with nasturtium flowers to serve.

Lime/Chocolate mint mojito Makes 1 glass

2 ½ tbsp lime juice
2 tsp cane sugar
4 tbsp white rum
3–4 stems of lemon or chocolate mint
crushed ice
soda

A recipe by Marta Meli-Czeburko

Add the sugar and lime juice to a tall glass and stir well.

Add the mint and crush gently to release the mint's ethereal oils.

Fill up the glass with crushed ice. You can also use ice cubes instead. Pour in the rum and stir briskly using a bar spoon so that the ingredients are thoroughly mixed.

Top up with soda water before serving and serve decorated with a slice of lime on the rim of the glass.

Ré's hedgehog slice with chocolate mint

One of our best-selling herbs of all time is our chocolate mint (*Mentha piperita var. piperita* or *Mentha piperita* "Multimentha"), both as a pot plant and as an ingredient in our café's hedgehog slice cake.

5 sprigs chocolate mint
3 tbsp dark cocoa powder
8 oz (250 g) coconut butter
3 eggs
3 tbsp sugar
24 butter cookies

Mill the chocolate mint a little and mix with 3 tablespoons of cocoa powder. Place in a closed jar and leave to marinate for 2–3 days.

Shake the chocolate mint, reserving the cocoa powder. Melt the coconut butter with the mint sprigs in a skillet over a low temperature, then remove the mint.

Cream the eggs and sugar together, add the cocoa powder, then stir in the melted coconut butter a little at a time.

Line a loaf pan with foil, then add alternate layers of butter cookies and cocoa mixture. Place in the refrigerator to chill and set.

Corsican mint or creeping mint (*Mentha requienii*) is another miniature mint with a chocolatey fragrance. We have it on the café tables in pots where customers cannot resist stroking it. It is often used for underplanting beneath sage, rosemary, or lavender.

Catnip or catmint (*Nepeta cataria*), lemon-scented catmint (*Nepeta cataria var. citriodora*), and dwarf catmint (*Nepeta fassenii oder mussinii*) are labiates and members of the mint family with the same beguiling mint scent. The many different, rather subtle aromas of the catnips were already popular with the ancient Romans long ago, and we must now try and find our way back towards rediscovering their passion for experimentation and their natural approach to these herbs.

As so often happens in my garden, plants or varieties pop up from time to time without any help from me. One day, I found lemon-scented catnip growing in various places, and I was bewitched by its intense lemon- or rather lime-scented aroma.

TIP   *When drying herbs, always pluck off the leaves and spread them out on a cloth in warm shade. This will help the aroma last longer than if dried on the stem. Sprigs of herbs hung upside down to dry are also liable to disintegrate more quickly.*

LEMON BALM
(Melissa officinalis)

I can remember there being large bushes of lemon balm and hyssop in our garden when I was six years old just after we had moved to Fronhofen. Presumably my mother had brought these plants along from our previous home. There was no ground elder in the garden at the time, as this was introduced, or found its way in, much later.

This lemon balm grew in the same spot for many decades, and we used it simply for tea. It is indeed one of the most undemanding of all herbs. Whether grown in the garden or cultivated on a balcony, it is always teeming with all kinds of insects. It increases by self-seeding and bushes out without becoming bare in the middle.

Lemon cake

4 eggs
scant 1 cup (200 g) sugar
salt
⅔ cup (150 g) butter
6 tbsp (100 g) crème fraîche
3¾ cups (400 g) flour
5 tsp baking powder
¾ cup (100 g) cornstarch
1 handful each of lemon-scented
catnip and/or lemon balm,
ground elder, dandelion, sorrel
juice and zest of 1 lemon
2¼ cups (250 g) confectioners' sugar
juice of 1 lemon
candied lemon slices, for decoration

Whisk the eggs, the sugar, and a pinch of salt until pale and frothy. Preheat the oven to 300 °F (150 °C).

Melt the butter over a very low heat, then mix with the crème fraîche into the egg mixture. Combine the flour, baking powder, and cornstarch, then sift into the mixture.

Wash, dry, and finely chop the herbs and stir into the cake batter along with the lemon juice and zest. Bake for approx. 1 hour in the pre-heated oven (carry out a skewer test).

Blend the confectioners' sugar and lemon juice into a smooth paste. Once the cake has cooled, spread this icing over the top and decorate with candied lemon slices.

CRETAN LEMON BALM
(Melissa officinalis altissima) Lamiaceae

Once I had really become hooked on the idea of herbs as the basis of various culinary dishes, I became interested in exploring the finer points of individual varieties. I became increasingly aware of the many variations in leaf shape, fragrance, and color. And this was how Cretan lemon balm, with its intense aroma and flavor of mandarins, came to my attention. Sometimes, herbs can be growing for years in my tender care before eventually being tried out in a dish as the result of someone's suggestion. In this case, it was a mandarin sorbet which finally led me to experiment with Cretan lemon balm in the kitchen.

Citrus tart à la Marguerite

Put the flour, butter, eggs, sugar, and orange zest in a bowl, then knead well with both hands. Cover and leave to chill in a cool place for 1 hour.

Peel the citrus fruit and cut into 1cm-thick slices. Grease a shallow flan dish, roll out three-quarters of the pastry, and line the flan dish, pressing the pastry down gently. Spread the marmalade over the fresh pastry.

Pre-heat the oven to 355 °F (180 °C). Sprinkle the Cretan lemon balm leaves over the jam. Arrange the sliced citrus fruit over the top. Roll out the rest of the pastry and cut into strips, arranging them in a lattice pattern over the sliced fruit. Bake in the pre-heated oven for 35–50 minutes.

2⅓ cups (270 g) spelt flour
9 tbsp (135 g) butter
4 eggs
5 tbsp (70 g) sugar
zest of half an orange
¾ cup (200 g) orange marmalade or sea buckthorn jam
8 mandarin oranges, 4 oranges, or
2 grapefruits
Cretan lemon balm leaves, or lemon balm, lemon thyme, lemon winter savory, lemon grass, or lemon verbena

Wild herb tortilla

Boil the potatoes, drain, and leave to cool in a colander. Finely chop and fry the onion in a skillet in a little oil. Add the potatoes, cut into small chunks.

Beat the eggs and season with salt and pepper. Blend in the finely chopped herbs and add to the vegetables in the skillet, mixing thoroughly.

Cover and cook over a low heat.

gen. 1 lb (500 g) potatoes
1 large onion
olive oil, for frying
6 eggs
3–4 bunches of wild herbs or any garden herbs of choice, but
including chives and parsley
salt, pepper

DECOLORANS OR SWEET YARROW fresh
nutmeg and cardamom *(Achillea decolorans) Asteraceae*

Although this culinary cousin of common yarrow does indeed smell and taste of nutmeg and cardamom, these are only its two most distinctive aromas. We still have not fully discovered all the secrets of this outwardly unprepossessing plant.

Its flavor also includes a hint of tarragon or wormwood as well as a touch of walnut. Even if you do not want to use it for culinary purposes, it still makes a charming, modest, and, above all, fragrant ground-cover plant. However, for it to survive in the garden, it must be kept free from invasive other herbs. Nor does it like long, hard frosts. On the other hand, it is easy to propagate thanks to its habit of putting out shoots, and it can also be cultivated in pots on a windowsill, especially as you will only need to use a small amount of this highly aromatic herb at any one time.

Cherry cake with sweet yarrow VEGAN

2 ripe bananas
1⅓ cups (150 g) sugar
½ cup (100 g) margarine
⅔ cup (150 ml) oat milk
3½ tbsp (50 ml) cherry juice
2 cups (200 g) ground almonds or cashews
2½ cups (300 g) spelt flour
cream of tartar baking powder
(use maker's instructions)
3 tbsp cocoa
10 oz (300 g) fresh pitted cherries, chokeberries, or other fruit
approx. 2 large stems or 1 handful of yarrow leaves

Cream the bananas, sugar, and margarine together until light and frothy, then add the milk and juice.

Pre-heat the oven to 355 °F (180 °C). Combine the flour and baking powder, then, using a large spoon, stir in the ground almonds, banana mixture, cocoa, and fruit.

Grease a cake pan with butter and dust with flour. Pour in the cake mixture and bake for about 1 hour in a pre-heated oven. Leave to cool in the oven—or enjoy while it is still warm!

Cocoa and coffee liqueur with sweet yarrow
Makes 1 quart (1 liter)

Place all the ingredients in a carafe or clean, dry bottle with a tight-fitting stopper. Crack any very large pieces of the rock candy, if necessary.

Leave to steep at room temperature for at least 1 week until the rock candy sugar has completely dissolved. Shake the bottle each day.

Strain the liqueur through a coffee filter into a carafe or decanter.

Serve chilled in a tumbler with ice and garnished with orange zest or warm in a liqueur glass with a topping of whipped cream.

⅓ cup (50 g) cocoa nibs (finely crushed and roasted cocoa beans)
½ cup (30 g) espresso beans
5 oz (150 g) brown rock candy sugar
1 quart (1 l) vodka
1 vanilla bean
4 sprigs of yarrow
peel from half an orange

A recipe by Marta Meli-Czeburko

Basic: syrup
Makes approx. 1½ quarts (1½ liters)

Soak the flower petals overnight in apple juice or water with the sugar.

A day or two later, bring to a boil and simmer for 10 minutes. Filter the flowers through a sieve, then reheat the liquid.

Transfer to bottles while still hot and close with a screw-top lid.

100 scarlet bee balm flowers
1 quart (1 l) water or apple juice
scant 1 cup (200 g) sugar

Variation
The following types of flowers can also be used instead of bee balm:
50 roses
30 umbrels of elderberry blossom
1 bunch dried woodruff
50 dandelion flowers (only the yellow ones)
300 violets (petals only)

NASTURTIUM

(Tropaeolum) Tropaeolaceae

It is now about time we looked at the nasturtium. In summer it suddenly starts to grow very quickly, and I usually find I have underestimated the amount of space it needs. It is such an attractive plant with its circular leaves, which can grow to large proportions, and its brightly colored flowers, which give off the combined aroma of cress and radish at the slightest touch. I often use garlands of nasturtiums for table decorations or fill tubs with them all around the garden. They also do very well as a provider of shade at the base of taller plants to prevent them drying out. Their large leaves also serve as the basis for my breakfast platters. The flowers can also be used to provide a decorative as well as a tasty splash of color, either as a garnish to round off a soup or as the crowning glory to a bowl of herb-flavored quark.

TIP   *To make nasturtium capers, take the unopened buds or fresh, green seeds and pickle them in vinegar.*

Basic: homemade capers   **VEGAN**

1 cup of buds or seeds
1½ cups good-quality vinegar
2 cups water
salt and sugar to taste

Season with any herbs of your choice, either leaving them in the cooking liquid or removing them after cooking.

Rinse the jars in hot water and leave to dry. Wash and dry the buds or seeds.

Boil the ingredients together for approx. 15 minutes, then transfer to the prepared jars and firmly screw the lids shut.

The buds or seeds should be just covered with liquid. Leave to marinate thoroughly for approx. 4–6 weeks before eating.

TIP   *Capers can also be made using dandelion, daisy, or plantain buds as well as nasturtium buds and seeds.*

ANISE HYSSOP Agastache

(Agastache foeniculum) Lamiaceae

Agastache, also known as anise hyssop, is a sturdy plant with a minty, bittersweet, hyssop-like aroma with distinct overtones of anise or fennel. It flowers until late summer, and its leaves and flowers may be harvested at any time. Not only does its aroma remain stable when cooked, but the leaves also make a decorative garnish. It is not only a lovely ornamental plant for the garden but also attracts large numbers of insects.

Last but not least, prolific cousins from North America:
SCARLET BEEBALM, MONARDA, BERGAMOT

(Monarda didyma) Lamiaceae

These labiates from North America make a delightful addition to any garden. Known as scarlet bee balm, bergamot, or monarda, these plants are greatly prized in our garden both as bedding plants and for use in tea. They are generally winter hardy and spread slowly by means of underground shoots. With their wonderful flowers and fragrance, they provide a lovely splash of summer in the herb bed. I have tried several different varieties, but my favorite remains the deep-red *Monarda didyma* which we use for herbal tea and which has a delicate flavor of Earl Grey. Its red flowers can also be made into an intensely aromatic and bright red syrup, or used as an ingredient in various fruit spreads.

TIP   *There are innumerable varieties of both bee balm and agastache, and their aromatic properties and color can vary greatly, so that the scope for experimentation both in gardening and culinary terms is considerable.*

Spotlight on the extravagant and unusual:

fall herbs

Occasional visitors from Japan, Korea, or Taiwan are always delighted to find a little reminder of home in my wild garden: Japanese herbs and their native cousins, for example, shiso, mitsuba (Japanese parsley), tade (Japanese water pepper), or wasabi. On the one hand, our guests are always surprised by the combination of the exotic and familiar in our garden and, on the other hand, encouraged to take a closer interest in this unfamiliar world. It is exactly the same for me when I travel to a foreign country. The plants offer me a very natural opportunity to get to know the new country, especially if I recognize any family relationships, for example, purely in the botanical sense.

SHISO OR PERILLA

(Perilla frutescens) Lamiaceae

Although shiso is one of a long list of culinary labiates, in Japan it plays a leading role as a kitchen herb. Its importance is roughly on a par with that of basil in our part of the world and is probably used as commonly as parsley here as an everyday flavoring. According to my Japanese friends, there is no dish which does not include shiso, and it can be used in every conceivable way. Because I am quite enchanted by its red-leaved appearance, I naturally became hooked very quickly on perilla, also known as black horehound. Unfortunately, shiso, like basil, only performs for about six months. It does, however, self-seed freely and will grow again the following year, outdoors, in a greenhouse, or on a balcony, with red, green, or variegated leaves.

Its flavor is described as minty, but red perilla is mainly distinctive because of its cumin aroma. Its green sister is similarly aromatic, although much naturally depends on location. In my view, they do not just parody the aromas of other herbs but also have an entirely unique identity of their own. Both go well with pumpkin and other hearty dishes. Baby shiso leaves have been a familiar ingredient in the world of gourmet cuisine for some time. One major Dutch plant nursery came up with a very effective idea and began marketing any easily cultivatable herbs as little "cresses." Now young shiso seedlings, which can be bought like cress in a carton, are simply called shiso cress. A real brainwave! Young borage seedlings are called borage cress and miniature lemon basil is lemon cress, or something along those lines. In this way, old favorites in company with various exotic newcomers are finding their way back or being quietly introduced by the back door into the world of fine cuisine.

Sushi with shiso `VEGAN`

1 cup (250 g) sushi rice
large bunch of garlic chives
1 tbsp soy sauce
20 large shiso leaves, 10 with stems attached
salt, pepper

Cook the rice, then leave to cool.

Wash and dry the herbs, then finely chop them with the garlic chives. Mix the herbs and rice together and season with soy sauce, salt, and pepper.

Mold the rice mixture into little balls, place each one on a shiso leaf with its stem removed, then wrap it in the leaf with its stem attached. Secure the stem.

Grilled sea bass—Loup de mer Serves 4

Fillet the fish, if bought whole, and descale. Peel and roughly chop the garlic cloves. Strip the needles off the rosemary, then chop. Lay the fish in oil and add the orange zest, rosemary, and garlic. Place in the refrigerator to marinate for about 3 hours.

To make the vinaigrette, peel and finely dice the shallot. Finely chop all the herbs and combine all the remaining ingredients using a hand-held electric blender. Add the chopped herbs and diced shallot, then season with salt, pepper, and sugar, to taste.

Remove the fish from the marinade, season with salt and pepper, and cook on the oiled metal grill of a barbecue. Drizzle the vinaigrette over the cooked fish.

4 sea bass fillets
salt, pepper

For the marinade

2 garlic cloves
3 large sprigs rosemary
zest of 1 orange
olive oil

For the vinaigrette

1 shallot
1 handful each of Japanese water pepper,
sorrel, nasturtium, green santolina
zest of ½ orange
1 tsp mustard
3 tbsp fish or vegetable stock
2 tbsp balsamic vinegar
3 tbsp olive oil from the fish marinade
salt, pepper, sugar

A recipe by Sascha Daniels

TADE OR JAPANESE WATER PEPPER
(Polygonum hydropiper fastigiatum) Polygonaceae

Tade is very similar in appearance to our own native water pepper and could easily share the culinary limelight with the latter if we could find it growing wild in moist semishade. My Japanese friends tell me that although tade is used for culinary purposes, it is regarded as an invasive weed which plagues the rice paddies. It just grows and spreads dramatically from year to year. It germinates masses of seeds in the greenhouse, always in the same spot, so that all I need to do to increase and harvest it is virtually just thin out the seedlings.

Its attractive leaves, tinged with red and green, are a culinary delight, and the crisp, spicy hot flavor of the leaves is a serious rival for chili. However, the hot taste quickly dissipates once in the mouth and almost certainly does not cause any stomach problems.

TIP *Planted along pond margins, it adds beautiful color accents and provides shade for other pond plants. It will probably germinate naturally the following year in exactly the same place. Tade grows equally well in garden soil or, provided it is well watered, in a pot, ideally on its own if it is to flourish as a solo specimen.*

Sushi with Japanese water pepper

¾ cup (200 g) sushi rice
salt, sugar
rice vinegar
3 sprigs of Japanese water pepper
2 tbsp yogurt

A recipe by Sascha Daniels

Prepare the sushi rice according to the instructions on the packet, then set aside to cool.

Remove the flowers and leaves from the Japanese water pepper. Blanch the leaves briefly in boiling water, then dry on a paper towel.

Mix the cooled sushi rice with the yogurt and Japanese water pepper flowers.

Wrap up portions of rice in the leaves and serve cold.

A natural yogurt and lemon dip makes an ideal accompaniment to this dish.

Two more exotics for the garden and palate:

VIETNAMESE CILANTRO
(Polygonum odoratum) Polygonaceae

I am very fortunate in that I can always fall back on two delightful garden and pond-margin plants if I do not happen to have any normal cilantro available. Vietnamese cilantro, which can also be cultivated in a pot, is a relative of tade and the rest of the knotweed family. Despite being a perennial, it does not like frost or dry conditions. A single plant will be enough to provide all the intensely aromatic leaves you might need for flavoring purposes.

VAP CA
(Houttuynia cordata) Saururaceae

Vap ca or the chameleon plant with its colorful foliage is another exotic native to Asia. You will find it marketed under the latter name in good garden centers, where it is sold as an ornamental plant. Vap ca is a modest but tenacious plant for the garden or, better still, a pond-marginal plant. Its flavor is reminiscent of lemon and cilantro. Its colorful foliage makes it a very attractive addition to the garden.

Cilantro and polenta slices   Makes approx. 10 slices

Bring the vegetable stock to a boil and add the polenta. Stir for 2 minutes, then leave to cool before adding the margarine.

Pre-heat the oven to 300 °F (150 °C). Finely chop the herbs, stir them into the mixture once it has cooled, and season to taste.

Transfer the mixture to a square ovenproof dish and bake in the oven for approx. 30 minutes until the mixture comes away easily from the side of the dish. Tip the baked mixture out of the dish and cut into slices.

1¼ cups (300 ml) vegetable stock
¾ cup (100 g) polenta
1 handful each of cilantro leaves, chives, parsley
salt, pepper, nutmeg
2 tbsp margarine

WASABI

(Wasabia japonica) Brassicaceae

Wasabi, an increasingly well-known figure on the culinary stage, is actually only a green pseudonym for the hot, spicy root of the plant, which is familiar to us as a seasoning for crisps, a coating for nuts, or in the form of a green paste. It can actually be cultivated very easily wherever we wish—in the garden, in a greenhouse, or on a balcony or windowsill. Unfortunately, the snails always manage to beat me to its lovely big leaves and in my opinion, even if the root remains undamaged, that will in the long run weaken the plants, which, no matter how undemanding they may be, would ultimately prefer to be growing alongside a Japanese mountain stream. Wasabi loses its complex and hot, spicy aromas very quickly once freshly grated. For this reason it is well worth cultivating it yourself—as wasabi can be far more than just a hot spice! Its large rounded fleshy leaves are reminiscent of the shape of its European relative, garlic mustard. It might surprise you to discover that its creamy leaves are more cabbage-flavored than hot. I usually wrap my vegan sushis either in shiso or wasabi leaves.

PEPPERWEED

(Lepidium latifolium) Brassicaceae

Although this native cousin of wasabi currently has a more minor role among the cast of culinary herbs, it is well on the way to greater celebrity. We still find it undiscovered on European coasts as well as along river banks, for example, along the Moselle. It is also regularly found in gardens, where, despite its widespread subterranean meanderings, it still leaves plenty of room for the other plants. It is not suitable for cultivating individually in a pot, as it would soon become root-bound and dry out.

Once established, however, it can be indulged as much as you like without coming to harm. You will notice that the flavor of its leaves is actually very reminiscent of wasabi, which is why we sometimes call this plant our native wasabi.

Pepperweed pesto **VEGAN**

½ cup (120 ml) olive oil
3½ tbsp (40 g) pine nuts
thumb-length piece of fresh ginger root
large pinch of salt
1 bunch pepperweed (without stems)

A recipe by Jens Stempel

Peel and finely chop the ginger. Using a food mixer or hand-held blender, purée the olive oil, ginger, salt, and coarsely chopped pepperweed into a pesto. Add the pine nuts and give them no more than a brief mix to make sure they do not disintegrate.

Transfer the pesto to small jars with screw-top lids, top with olive oil, and seal tightly. The pesto will keep in the refrigerator for several days.

Intermezzo with chives and friends

The first herbs to awaken our sleepy, hibernating spirits in early spring are field garlic and bear's garlic, quickly followed by the early shoots of chives and garlic. However, the leaves of onion plants (*Allium cepa*), whether white, red, or yellow, and shallots (*Allium ascalonium*), which will be ready to harvest in the fall of their first year, can also be used like giant chives. The onions are normally harvested in late summer. The leaves of Egyptian tree onion (*Allium cepa var. Viviparum*) and Welsh onion (*Allium fistulosum*), on the other hand, can be enjoyed all year round, while garden leeks and wild leeks (*Allium ampeloprasum, syn.: Allium porrum*), of which the whole plant is edible, is ready to harvest in the fall.

WILD OR FIELD GARLIC
(Allium vineale)

The first glimpses of wild garlic's delicate little tube-like leaves can be seen in spring as you admire the dark bluish-green shimmering grass on a sloping bank. You may even have already missed spotting it in vine-yards or even in your own garden, as once happened to me. I suddenly spotted it growing there, after which I began to look after it, that is to say, I steer the lawn mower around it. The plant has now spread even farther and its delicate stems have colonized the ground beneath the pear tree. Although the stalks are very delicate, wild garlic is crunchier than chives, a close relative, and as well as producing flowers it also develops minia-ture onions, which can be eaten or planted to increase the stock.

FIELD GARLIC
(Allium oleraceum)

Similar in appearance to its smaller cousin, garlic chives, field garlic has tube-like leaves which tend to be rather concave on one side and bigger as a whole. It can be found more or less throughout the whole of Europe. A friend of mine once gave me a few bulbs of the plant. It took an immediate liking to my garden, appropriated a few patches of ground, and now continues to spread happily. Consequently, I can afford now and again to dig up entire plants, complete with bulbs, to diversify our menu. As a general principle, both of these plants can be used like chives, and whereas garlic chives include a hint of garlic, the flavor of field garlic is more reminiscent of leek.

GARLIC CHIVES
(Allium tuberosum)

Garlic chives, widely used in Asia, have very flat leaves, which can be harvested all year round. With its delicate garlic flavor, this is my favorite herb for seasoning my sushi creations. It is also wonderfully easy to cultivate in pots, is frost hardy, and flowers like bear's garlic, which also produces edible flowers.

TIP   *All flowers produced by herbs are edible and will enhance culinary dishes with their variety of flavors.*

Focaccia with green santolina or curry plant

Makes approx. 10 portions

Dissolve the yeast in a little lukewarm water. Add the remaining water, oil, and salt, then add the flour and knead all the ingredients together. Leave to prove in a warm place for 30 mins.

Pre-heat the oven to 390 °F (200 °C). Knead the dough once more, then shape into 8–10 flat rounds.

Press the olives into the dough base, then sprinkle with green santolina, or chopped curry plant or rosemary, and salt. Drizzle with olive oil and bake for 10–15 minutes in the pre-heated oven.

Green santolina will intensify the hearty flavor of focaccia, while curry plant can be finely chopped and kneaded into the dough. The latter is one of my personal favorites, and I always use a whole handful of herbs in each focaccia.

For the base
½ cube or 1 sachet of yeast
2½ cups (300 g) spelt flour
½ cup (100 ml) water, more if necessary
5 tbsp olive oil
1 tbsp sea or rock salt

For the topping
olives, pitted
green santolina, curry plant, or,
for traditional focaccia, rosemary
2 tbsp olive oil
salt

HYSSOP
(Hyssopus officinalis) Lamiaceae

As with common rue, there has always been a bit of a culinary cloud hanging over hyssop even though it was very popular with the ancient Romans. In the garden, it provides a veritable paradise for insects with its attractive deep-blue, white, or pink flowers. I think my mother told me that it was traditionally used in meat dishes, and its healing properties convinced me that I could use it in pulse dishes or to add a tangy flavor to sweet jams. I always associate its strong and multifaceted aroma, which is tart and somehow a bit dark, with forest smells, and I would recommend it without hesitation for game dishes.

"Quince power" Makes approx. 10 jars (7 oz/200 g each) **VEGAN**

Wash and halve the quinces. Bring to a boil in a steamer along with the sea buckthorn, hyssop, and a little water. Once the water has evaporated, press the ingredients through a sieve.

Measure out a quantity of juice, then add the appropriate amount of preserving sugar, according to the package instructions. Pour the hot mixture into jars and close with screw-top lids. Hyssop will add an extra hint of fruity, spicy flavor to this fruit spread.

4 lb (1.8 kg) quince
8 oz (200 g) sea buckthorn
5 sprigs hyssop
preserving sugar

Hyssop and lentil salad **VEGAN**

Rinse the lentils, then put in a large pan with all the water. Add the bay leaf and thyme and bring to the boil, then reduce the heat and simmer, uncovered, until the lentils are tender (about 20–30 minutes).

Drain off the water, set aside the lentils to cool, and remove the bay leaf and thyme. Finely dice the onions. Slice the mushrooms. Gently fry both ingredients, then leave to cool.

Finely chop the herbs. Mix all the ingredients together, season with salt and green peppers, and add the vinegar and oil.

Finally, carefully add the drained mandarin oranges. Serve the salad garnished with edible flowers.

18 oz (500 g) brown lentils
2 quarts (2 l) water
1 bay leaf
3 sprigs thyme
1 red and 1 white onion
1½ cups (100 g) button mushrooms
1 tbsp green peppers, pickled
salt, vinegar, oil
1 handful each of fresh hyssop,
lovage, parsley, chives
1 small can mandarin oranges
edible flowers, to garnish

LEMON VERBENA

(Aloysia citrodora, Syn.: Aloysia triphylla) Verbenaceae

Whenever I wander through my greenhouse in summer, the lemon verbena reminds me every day of its fresh, sweet presence. Since it grows right beside the path, one cannot help brushing against its arching branches in passing and becoming enveloped in its unmistakable lemon fragrance.

A native of South America, lemon verbena needs some basic protection in winter. However, it can happily be left to over-winter in a cold room and will then leave you waiting a long time until it reappears in late May. A very popular herb in France, vervain, as it is known there, usually simply sprouts brand new shoots, producing an abundant harvest far into the fall. During the past few years, I have been trying it out in all kinds of different dishes which can benefit from its intense lemon aroma. It is a classic ingredient in an evening glass of tea, but I also use it in all my tomato sauces. Lemon verbena is a real all-rounder which can be added to cold drinks and desserts or used to round off the flavor of smoothies and fruit spreads.

Quince crisp

For the quince filling
4 quinces
1 handful of lemon verbena
scant ½ cup (100 g) sugar
1¼ cups (300 ml) apple juice
½ cup (100 ml) orange juice
½ cup (100 ml) dry Riesling

For the crisp topping
scant ½ cup (100 g) sugar
gen. ⅓ cup (200 g) flour
1 cup (100 g) oat flakes
1 tsp ground cinnamon
1½ sticks (180 g) butter (at room temperature)

For the fruit drink
quince cooking liquid
small amount of lemon verbena

A recipe by Sascha Daniels

To make the quince filling, caramelize the sugar in a saucepan. Add the wine, apple juice, and orange juice. Finely chop the lemon verbena and add to the saucepan. Leave to marinate overnight.

The next day, peel the quinces, cut into quarters, and remove the cores. Dice the fruit into small cubes.

Strain the lemon verbena from the liquid in which it was marinated, then simmer the quince in the same liquid until soft.

Pre-heat the oven to 390 °F (200 °C). To make the crumble topping for the crisp, combine all the ingredients and knead into a dough, then crumble it onto a baking sheet. Bake in the pre-heated oven for 20–30 minutes or until crisp. Serve warm with the stewed quince.

Mix the quince marinade with a little fresh lemon verbena and serve the drink with the crisp.

Beef rib steak with apricot and lemon verbena sauce and herb potatoes Serves 2

Pre-heat the oven to 250 °F (120 °C). Wrap the herbs around the beef, securing them with kitchen twine. Season with plenty of salt and sear quickly with the butter on both sides in a hot ovenproof skillet. Peel and slice the shallots and add to the skillet.

Arrange the rib steak on the shallots and cook in the pre-heated oven for approx. 10 minutes until the core temperature is approx. 118–120 °F (48–50 °C). Switch off the oven, open the oven door, and leave the meat to rest for 10–12 minutes.

To make the herb potatoes, finely chop half the herbs. Put the rest of the herbs with the potatoes in a saucepan with water, season with salt to taste, bring to the boil, and simmer until tender.

To make the fruit sauce, place the apricot slices in a saucepan. Add the sugar, and mix with the apricots along with the orange juice. Simmer all the ingredients at a rapid boil for 3–4 minutes until it thickens.

Cut the lemon verbena into thin strips and add to the apricot mixture once it has finished cooking. Season with salt and pepper.

Reheat the rib steak briefly in the butter left in the skillet on both sides.

Melt the cubed butter in a saucepan, then add the chopped herbs and toss the boiled potatoes in the mixture.

Serve the beef with the potatoes, drizzling a little herb butter over the top. Serve with the apricot accompaniment.

For the rib steak

14 oz (400 g) rib steak, cut in 2 slices
½ lb (200 g) shallots
4 sprigs thyme
1 sprig rosemary
4 leaves of Japanese water pepper
2 tsp sea salt
¾ stick (80 g) butter, cubed

For the herb potatoes

1 bunch each of French sorrel, parsley, basil, sweet cicely, and chervil
4 leaves of Japanese water pepper
gen. 1 lb (500 g) small waxy potatoes
½ stick (50 g) butter, cubed

For the fruit sauce

gen. 1 lb (500 g) apricots, sliced
¾ cup (200 ml) orange juice
scant ½ cup (100 g) sugar
3 tbsp preserving sugar
½ bunch lemon verbena
salt, pepper

A recipe by Michael Daus

TIP   *The temperature in the center of the rib steak should be between 118 and 120 °F (48 and 52 °C).*

Lamb shank with pumpkin and honey risotto and lemon verbena juice Serves 4

4 lamb shanks
2 medium onions
3 carrots
¼ celery root
1 leek (white part only)
3 tbsp butter, melted
1 tbsp tomato paste
1 cup (250 ml) red wine
2 cups (500 ml) lamb stock
1 Hokkaido pumpkin
olive oil
1½ cups (300 g) risotto rice
1 cup (250 ml) white wine
1 bay leaf
3¼ cups (750 ml) vegetable stock
approx. 10 leaves lemon verbena
2 tbsp mascarpone
½ cup (50 g) Parmesan, freshly grated
2 tbsp clear honey
ground ivy, to garnish
cornstarch, if necessary
salt, pepper, and mace

A recipe by Freddy Bürkle

Rinse the lamb shanks, pat dry, and remove any sinews.

Peel and roughly chop one onion. Wash and roughly chop the carrots, celery root, and leek.

Pre-heat the oven to 340 °F (170 °C). Heat the melted butter in a flame-proof dish and sear the lamb quickly on all sides. Remove the lamb from the dish, add the vegetables, and cook until lightly browned. Stir in the tomato paste and cook for a few more minutes. Pour in the red wine and lamb stock to dissolve any browned residue in the dish. Season the lamb with salt and pepper, arrange side by side in the dish and cook in the pre-heated oven for about one and a half hours.

Meanwhile, peel and finely dice the second onion. Remove the core, stalk, and seeds from the pumpkin, then cut into chunks, reserving some for a garnish. Heat a little olive oil in a saucepan, add the pumpkin and onions, and sweat until translucent. Add the rice and continue to cook a little longer. Add the wine and bay leaf and bring to the boil.

Gradually add 3 cups (700 ml) vegetable stock, stirring constantly, until the rice has reached the desired texture after about 20 minutes. Remove from the heat.

When the meat begins to come away from the bone, remove it from the sauce, wrap in aluminum foil, and keep warm in the switched-off oven.

Strain the sauce through a sieve, then cook over a high heat until the liquid is reduced. If you want to speed things up a bit, stir in a little corn-starch to thicken the sauce. Add the lemon verbena, season with salt and pepper to taste, and continue to cook over a low heat.

Heat up the risotto with the rest of the vegetable stock over a low heat. Stir in the mascarpone and Parmesan and season to taste with salt, pep-per, mace, and honey. Sauté the reserved pumpkin in a little olive oil and season with salt and pepper.

TIP   *At 167 °F/75 °C the meat will be pink on the inside; at 176 °F/80 °C or more it will be well done. If you have enough time, the lamb can be cooked overnight at 176 °F/80 °C for 10–12 hours for extra tenderness.*

CURRY PLANT AND GREEN SANTOLINA

(Helichrysum italicum) Asteraceae and (Santolina viridis) Asteraceae

My café clientele, garden visitors, and herb customers have been enjoying this silvery-gray curry plant and bright green santolina for many years. Both herbs are native to more southern climes but are equally easy to grow in the garden and will thrive on a balcony or windowsill, where they can develop into bushy plants. Since only a small amount of each herb will be sufficient to add a distinctive flavor to any dish, a single plant will be enough to cover all your needs.

Their names speak for themselves and so the curry plant should season a real curry occasionally, and it is entirely natural for green santolina to add flavor to focaccia bread. We use the latter's fresh, tender stems, kneading them, finely chopped, into the dough for our santolina rolls or add them, finely chopped, to stewed tomatoes.

Olive muffins Makes 12 muffins

Wash, dry, and finely chop the herbs the day before they are needed. Mix the herbs and cream together and leave overnight.

Blend together the ingredients for the muffins, then add the herbs-and-cream mixture prepared the previous day. Pre-heat the oven to 300 °F (150 °C). Fill the muffin molds with the mixture and top each one with half an olive. Bake in the pre-heated oven for approx. 30 minutes. Carry out a skewer test.

Warning: *Please see advice on rue on page 72.*

1 handful of green santolina, fennel, rue
2 tbsp cream

For the muffins
1¼ cups (180 g) flour
1 tsp baking powder
½ cup (50 g) Parmesan
salt
3 eggs
½ cup (⅛ l) milk
scant ½ cup (100 g) butter
olives, to decorate

Green santolina rolls

Knead the flour, yeast, sugar, pinch of salt, and liquid into a yeasty dough. Cover and leave to prove in a warm place for approx. 30 minutes.

Wash, dry, pick over, and strip the leaves off the green santolina. Finely chop the tiny narrow leaves and knead into the dough.

Divide the dough into small portions, place in molds, and leave to prove once more.

Pre-heat the oven to 300 °F (150 °C) and bake the bread rolls for about 30 minutes.

Basic: yeast dough
3½ cups (500 g) flour
½ cube of yeast; if using dry yeast, check maker's instructions
1 tsp sugar
pinch of salt
1 cup warm milk or water
1 handful of green santolina

When green seems even greener…

winter herbs

The following herbs will provide a fresh green boost to dark winter days. However, they do require quite a lot of space for themselves as, even assuming they manage to survive snow, icy winds, and even frost, we still need enough of them to harvest in the quantities we need. We can also highly recommend these herbs for cultivating in a greenhouse, if you are fortunate enough to have one.

CORN SALAD
(Valerianella locusta) Valerianaceae

One of the easiest winter herbs to cultivate is corn salad, also known as lamb's lettuce, which nowadays is available all year round. And I must admit that for the past few years, I too have been growing it both in the garden and in the greenhouse on an all-year-round basis. I can always find a few specimens popping up between the other herbs, and the sight of this delicate, creamy little herb never fails to give me a nice warm feeling. I feel hugely protective toward this tiny little member of the valerian family whenever I see it shooting up all over the place, growing tirelessly, year in, year out. And yet things are actually the other way round in so far as I am the one who benefits from the deep sense of calm which I derive from its faithful companionship and from knowing that I can always rely on its presence. It almost hurts me in summer to have to cut back its lush growth to give the surrounding plants a bit more space. However, this is the way to guarantee continuity, and I never have to propagate it by sowing seeds, as I can always rely on plenty of little rosettes of this herb continuing to grow through the winter.

Maiga's pumpkin pie

For the short pastry base
1¾ cups (250 g) flour
½ cup + 1 tbsp (125 g) butter
3½ tbsp (50 g) sugar
salt
1 egg

For the filling
1 Hokkaido pumpkin (approx. 1 lb/500 g)
4 eggs
salt
scant ½ cup (100 g) sugar
1 cup (100 g) ground almonds, cashews, or walnuts
2 tbsp spelt flour
1 bunch of fresh shiso and/or sweet yarrow, although Japanese water pepper is also delicious

Mix the ingredients for the short pastry base into a smooth dough, then set aside in a cool place until you have prepared the filling.

Remove the seeds from the pumpkin, but leave it unpeeled. Either bake in the oven or cook in a saucepan of water until tender. Purée the cooked pumpkin into a fine paste using an electric hand-held blender. Alternatively, dice the pumpkin into small cubes and fry briefly in butter, then add a little wine or water and simmer until tender.

Finely chop the fresh herbs.

Pre-heat the oven to 390 °F (200 °C). Separate the eggs. Cream the egg yolks and 6 tablespoons (80 g) of the sugar until light and frothy. Carefully stir in the puréed pumpkin, almonds, herbs, or spices. Whisk the egg whites, remaining sugar, and a pinch of salt until stiff, then fold into the egg-yolk mixture.

Roll out the pastry into a thin sheet a little larger than the spring-form pan. Line the base and sides of the pan with pastry to give the pie a high raised edge. Tip the pumpkin mixture onto the pastry base and bake for approx. 45 minutes at 390 °F (200°).

Serve on a plate and decorate with hyssop flowers, arugula, or the tips of thyme leaves.

PURSLANE

(Claytonia perfoliata or Montia perfoliata) Montiaceae

The first delicate little seed leaves appear in late summer or early fall, followed quite quickly by a typical spoon-shaped leaf. If I do not carefully thin out, transplant, pot up, or simply weed the seedlings immediately, I will be confronted soon afterward with a sea of millions of tiny purslane plants. Such abundance can be quite difficult to cope with, and yet it cannot fail to gladden a gardener's heart. I never really understand why we try and keep our fields and garden beds so bare, taking such care that nothing sets seed or has the audacity to decide to grow uninvited. I simply cannot get enough wild plants and sometimes get a bit carried away leaving them to grow at will—with the result that they often thrive so much in compost-enriched ground that they end up depriving one another of space. Even so—I find such abundance very heartening! And purslane's fresh, juicy flavor and creamy leaves are like a summer salad in the depths of winter!

CHICKWEED

(Stellaria media) Caryophyllaceae

Chickweed, with its numerous little spreading shoots, will cover and protect any open patches of garden as if it is trying to knit together open wounds. It keeps the soil moist and, like a living layer of mulch, prevents the soil from drying out or eroding. If you allocate a few moist areas of garden to chickweed, it will reward you by flourishing into lovely big plants which are easy to harvest. Since chickweed often grows in large clumps, it really is better to leave just a few plants standing and weed out the rest. The flavor is reminiscent of fresh young pea pods or corn cobs. We tend to use it mainly as a fresh salad ingredient. Chickweed goes particularly well with raw vegetable dishes.

Chickweed and beet salad VEGAN

Wash, peel, and grate the beets. Wash and pick over the chickweed.

Make a dressing by blending together the maple syrup, balsamic vinegar, oil, salt, and pepper to taste. Finely dice the onion and add to the dressing.

Mix in the grated beets, then sprinkle with chickweed.

4 small beets
1 handful chickweed
1 tbsp maple syrup
2 tbsp dark balsamic vinegar
1 tbsp oil
salt, pepper
1 red onion

CHERVIL the finest aromatic herb

(Anthriscus cerefolium) Apiaceae

Like all the winter herbs described here, chervil just propagates itself in late summer, both in the garden and in the greenhouse. It is also easy to grow on a windowsill. It is one of the essential ingredients in Frankfurt Green Sauce as it is in *fines herbes*. Its flavor, a combination of aniseed and carrot, its almost transparently delicate leaves, and its robust nature make this herb a very special favorite of mine. The lacy white umbrels of white flowers are also used for culinary purposes.

Carrot and ground elder cake or Carrot and chervil cake

4 eggs
pinch of salt
scant ½ cup (100 g) sugar
juice of half a lemon
zest from 1 unwaxed lemon
⅓ cup (50 g) each of flour, polenta, ground nuts, chopped walnuts, and cornstarch
1 tsp baking powder
½ lb (200 g) carrots
2 generous handfuls of young ground elder leaves or chervil
pinch each of cinnamon and ground cloves

Separate the eggs and whisk the whites with a pinch of salt until stiff. Beat the egg yolks, sugar, lemon juice, and citrus zest together until pale and creamy.

Pre-heat the oven to 300 °F (150 °C). Combine the flour, polenta, nut ingredients and cornstarch with the baking powder, then stir into the egg-yolk mixture. Grate the carrots and finely chop the ground elder or chervil leaves.

Stir both ingredients into the cake batter and season with the cinnamon and ground cloves. Fold in the egg whites and transfer the mixture to a greased spring-form pan.

Bake in the center of the pre-heated oven for approx. 1 hour.

BITTERCRESS or HERB BARBARA
(Barbarea vulgaris) Brassicaceae

Different varieties of bittercress, also known as Herb Barbara, are often seen growing around the edge of fields and are identifiable by their rosettes of oakleaf-shaped leaves. The plants can also be very dark green in color and juicy, depending on where they are growing. This wild herb can also find its way into gardens, and I myself have had a white and green variety in my own garden for many years. A few leaves of this combined with bloody or red-veined dock make a very attractive addition to a wild herb salad. With its long flowering period, it also provides a long-lasting splash of color in the garden, its abundance of yellow flowers attracting all kinds of insects. This herb can be very bitter and spicily hot if it gets too dry. One plant in the garden or on the balcony will be sufficient, and it makes a good companion plant to grow with peas and beans and all kinds of umbellifers, provided it is regularly treated with compost. I always use bittercress as an alternative to watercress, which is less easy to cultivate in a bed.

WATERCRESS home-grown peppery flavor
(Nasturtium officinale) Brassicaceae

Watercress is an aquatic or semi-aquatic plant, thriving best in ponds or flowing water, such as brooks and streams. However, it can also be grown in the garden, or you can keep a few plants going over winter in a damp, cold greenhouse or in tubs. If watered generously, it will reward you with plenty of leaves to harvest. Watercress is another of the traditional ingredients in Frankfurt Green Sauce, adding a very interesting peppery flavor.

Watercress soup `VEGAN`

Add the leek, carrot, lovage, bay leaf, salt, and pepper to the water and bring to the boil. Once the vegetables are tender, purée all the ingredients.

Finely dice the onion and sweat in oil until translucent. Stir in the flour and add the puréed vegetables.

Season to taste with nutmeg and bring to the boil. Sprinkle in the watercress, remove from the heat, and purée using a hand-held electric blender. Serve in soup mugs or bowls, add a dash of soy cream, and garnish with watercress leaves or flowers.

Variation: instead of spelt flour, use 1–2 potatoes, boiling them along with the other vegetables.

1½ quarts (1½ l) water
1 leek, 1 carrot
3 sprigs lovage
1 bay leaf
salt, pepper
1 onion
oil
2 tbsp spelt flour
4 handfuls watercress
nutmeg
soy cream
watercress, for decoration

SCURVY GRASS peppery vitamin bomb
(Cochlearia officinalis) Brassicaceae

Like buckshorn plantain, ice plant, and perennial arugula, scurvy grass, which is likewise a native of coastal regions, will appreciate a taste of sea salt occasionally. Scurvy grass was a popular herb in ancient times and widely used and cultivated until a few centuries ago, since when it has become one of the forgotten garden and culinary herbs. One of its most useful characteristics is that it grows in winter, providing a good source of vitamins and freshness. It resembles watercress in flavor but is slightly more bitter and peppery. Its white flowers have a strong scent of honey and are also edible. I can highly recommend this herb as an ingredient in a quark dip in winter, as a peppery seasoning for fatty dishes, as an ingredient in mixed salads, or as a source of winter greenery on the balcony.

WHITETOP OR HOARY CRESS a remarkable delicacy *(Draba muralis) Brassicaceae*

Whitetop is a real little gem, and I love this tiny plant not just as a salad ingredient but because it is an unfailing source of pleasure. When it germinates in late summer it is no bigger than a pin-head, yet it already has all the characteristics of a mature plant. It competes with arugula for the choicest spots and will grow to the same size whether in the greenhouse or in a pot. Whether you pick individual leaves or whole rosettes, the leaves seem to melt between your fingers. The surface of the leaves is slightly rough, a bit like a cat's tongue, but so delicate that you can certainly use all the leaves. Mix it with corn salad and a mild dressing, and get ready to discover some unfamiliar nuances of flavor! At first you will notice a hint of sweetness, followed by a really delicious peppery taste, and finishing with a sweet hint of woodruff. As far as I am concerned, whitetop is the most remarkable herb of all.

TIP   *Gardening enthusiasts will find whitetop a real asset as one of the various herbs which can be used to protect the ground in winter. These include corn salad, chickweed, scurvy grass, and purslane. Whitetop and scurvy grass also make excellent balcony plants and are ideal for planting underneath other plants in big tubs to be eaten and enjoyed throughout the winter!*

ARUGULA revival of a favorite herb: wall-rocket and annual arugula

(Diplotaxis tenuifolia/muralis or Rucola selvatica) and (Eruca sativa or cultiva)

Like basil and bear's garlic, arugula, also known as rocket, is still one of the most popular herbs. Mainly for the benefit of my beloved, I like to cultivate annual arugula (*Eruca sativa* or *cultiva*) as well as perennial wall-rocket or wild arugula (*Diplotaxis tenuifolia/muralis* or *Rucola selvatica*), which is meanwhile available everywhere. And why not, after all, considering that the ancient Romans were already enthusiastic fans of this robust member of the cabbage family? All we ever need do is cast our eyes back to antiquity to realize that our perception of food and agriculture has actually become rather limited. It is true, of course, that the Romans and Greeks also gleaned a good deal from the Arabian world and even farther afield and are even reputed to have wiped out some of the most popular herbs completely, with the result that they no longer exist for us to enjoy. I have to admit that I do admire their love of diversity and constant striving to discover new things. I am often aware in my seminars of a feeling of aversion to anything strange or unfamiliar. Herbs always seem to be tinged with a sense of something frightening or dangerous, and I hope that my little herb sessions can help open up the delicious world of herbs and make it more accessible.

ROADSIDE PENNYCRESS the best garlic ever!

(Thlaspi alliaceum or alliarum) Brassicaceae

And while we are on the subject of remarkable herbs—the cabbage family have some really interesting companions. Roadside pennycress is extremely easy to cultivate—I find it remarkable that it is still not available to buy!

We use this wonderful herb to add interest to mixed salads, as a topping on a pizza instead of arugula, or as an alternative to bear's garlic. Its extremely pleasant, very delicate garlic flavor with a hint of arugula and chives cannot fail to delight the taste buds and can be used to flavor all kinds of dishes.

TIP   *The flowers of all these members of the cabbage family are edible, as are the tender, green shoots, especially the nutty-flavored flowers of annual arugula.*

... a typical summer's day in Maiga's wild herb garden ...

Recipe authors

Marta Meli-Czeburko
Proprietor, Barfly
Aacher Strasse 7, 56841 Traben-Trarbach
www.barfly-online.de
barfly_online@hotmail.com

Sascha Daniels
Proprietor and chef de cuisine
Restaurant Cavallerie
Hauptstr. 30, 23936 Stepenitztal
saniels@icloud.com

Michael Daus
Chef de partie
Romantik Jugendstil Hotel Bellevue
An der Mosel 11, 56841 Trarbach
www.bellevue-hotel.de, michaeldaus@gmx.de

Katharina Schnabl
Kleinkost restaurant
Katharina Schnabl and Dennis Krömer
Lotter Strasse 113, 49078 Osnabrück
www.kleinkost.net

Jens Stempel
Proprietor and chef de cuisine
Landhaus Stempel
Hauptstrasse 32–33
55452 Windesheim
www.landhaus-stempel.de

Sebastian Schuff
Chef and manager
Gartenhotel Hunsrücker Fass
Hauptstrasse 70, 55758 Kempfeld
www.gartenhotel-hunsruecker-fass.de

About the authors

Katharina worked with us for a year in the wild herb garden and now runs the Kleinkost restaurant in Osnabrück with her partner. Freddy, Marta, Michael, and Sascha are friends and colleagues from the lovely Moselle town of Traben-Trarbach. Their creativity and passion for herbs have contributed to the variety of recipes and special highlights within this book. Jens and Sebastian are two young chefs from the Hunsrück who conjure up gourmet dishes from the abundance of regional produce.

Acknowledgements

Not only are these acknowledgements obligatory, but they truly come from the heart and reflect a genuine appreciation for all the support which I have received over the past 20 years. First and foremost, great credit must go to all the chefs for their commitment and for contributing their recipes: Katharina, Marta, Freddy, Jens, Michael, Sascha, and Sebastian.

Seduced by the aromatic world of herbs, I send my love and thanks to my parents, Ré and Richard, and my wonderful partner, Frank.

Just as my parents once helped me to discover the world of nature, I in turn always felt drawn to a greater or lesser degree to follow a path which would eventually lead me specifically into my chosen career. I would therefore like to extend my thanks in this respect to those who have also helped me financially.

Anne Untermann, who gave me my first book on culinary wild herbs, Heinrich Hüni, who enabled me to take a semester of leave, Anne Liller, my second mom and herb enthusiast par excellence. But ultimately it was my friends, Esther and Kerstin, who helped me get properly started in a career revolving around the diverse world of herbs. To all my customers, visitors, and friends of our wild herb garden, I would like to say a big thank you for your loyalty and friendly suggestions regarding our continued development—there is always more to learn!

And last but not least, my thanks to Martin Dort and Christine Paxmann and crew, who made this second book of herbs possible.

The author

Maiga Werner, born in 1966, always felt a very close connection to her parents' garden and to nature in general. After a career route which led her from philosophy to media design to work as a chef and gardener, she eventually found her way back to that garden of her childhood. This strong connection is the source of her inspiration and the answer to the question asked of her as a child about what she wanted to do when she grew up. Her aim, once quoted as a casual remark in the school newspaper, of becoming a farmer and writer obviously paved the way toward this objective and eventually resulted in the creation of the present-day wild herb garden. The fresh herbs from this garden are now distributed to gourmet chefs, and private epicures, and to produce organic pot herbs. These initial beginnings as a fresh herb supplier have blossomed into a flourishing herb paradise, which this book invites readers to explore for themselves as a culinary experience and which can also be visited in person.

Maiga Werner
Wild herb garden – words and herbs
Fronhofen 2
54483 Kleinich
www.naturkraeutergarten.de
www.naturkraeutergarten.com
www.wordsandherbs.de
DE ÖKO 006 Naturland member
maiga@naturkraeutergarten.de

Special recipes by Ré Werner, mother of the author

Recipe index

Index of herbs

Picture credits

Alexander Taube: 86 center, bottom, 101 top,
113 top, 114, 131 top, 136 bottom
Brigitte Werner: 93
Christine Paxmann: 8, 11, 15, 20, 61, 70, 77, 133
Katharina Schnabl: 140 (fourth picture from top)
Maja Twesten: U4 left, 16, 19, 23, 36, 39, 44, 47, 51, 57,
58, 74, 90, 105, 110, 116, 130, 134
Maiga Werner: U4 center, U4 right, 5 top left, bottom, 10,
12 both, 13 both, 17, 18, 21, 22, 25, 27, 28, 30, 31, 32, 33,
34, 35, 37, 38, 40, 41, 42, 43, 45, 46, 49, 50 both, 53, 54,
55, 56, 59, 62, 66, 67, 68 top, 69 all, 71, 72, 73, 75, 76, 78,
79 both, 85, 86 top, 89, 92, 95, 96, 97, 100, 101 bottom,
102, 104, 106, 108, 109, 111 both, 112 both, 113 bottom,
117, 118, 119, 120, 124, 125, 126, 128, 129, 131 bottom,
132, 135 both, 136 top, 137 both, 138, 140 (first to third
picture from top)
Marguerit Pollard: 64, 81, 94, 115
Marliese Pfeil: 7
Marta Meli-Czebruko: 98
Sarah Golbaz: 82
Shutterstock: U1
Sebastian Schnuff: 48, 140 bottom
Stockfood: 5 right, 24, 123
Timo Volz: 140 (fifth picture from top)

Abbreviations and Quantities

1 oz = 1 ounce = 28 grams
1 lb = 1 pound = 16 ounces 1
1 cup = approx. 5–8 ounces* (see below)
1 cup = 8 fl uid ounces = 250 milliliters (liquids)
2 cups = 1 pint (liquids) = 15 milliliters (liquids)
8 pints = 4 quarts = 1 gallon (liquids)
1 g = 1 gram = 1/1000 kilogram = 5 ml (liquids)
1 kg = 1 kilogram = 1000 grams = 2¼ lb
1 l = 1 liter = 1000 milliliters (ml) = 1 quart
125 milliliters (ml) = approx. 8 tablespoons = ½ cup
1 tbsp = 1 level tablespoon = 15–20 g* (depending on density)
= 15 milliliters (liquids)
1 tsp = 1 level teaspoon = 3–5 g * (depending on density) = 5 ml
(liquids)

*The weight of dry ingredients varies significantly depending on
the density factor, e.g. 1 cup of flour weighs less than 1 cup of
butter. Quantities in ingredients have been rounded up or down for
convenience, where appropriate. Metric conversions may therefore
not correspond exactly. It is important to use either American or
metric measurements within a recipe.

Disclaimer

The information and recipes printed in this book are provided to the best of our knowledge and belief and based on our own
experience, but they are not a substitute for personal consultation, examination, diagnosis, or treatment from a doctor, in
particular with regard to interactions with medicines that you may be taking, and in relation to age, allergies, pregnancy, or
breastfeeding. Please ensure that all plants, in particular those with a potent effect, are always used in exactly the amounts
stated. The information and recipes contained in this book are used at the reader's own risk. We assume no liability for the
accuracy or completeness of this information, or for any effects or adverse reactions that may occur. Neither the author nor the
publisher shall accept liability for any damage whatsoever which may arise directly or indirectly from the use of this book.
This disclaimer applies in particular to the use and consumption of untreated raw milk and/or raw milk products, which the
author and publisher strongly advise against due to the associated health risks. It is advisable not to serve dishes that contain
raw eggs to very young children, pregnant women, elderly people, or to anyone weakened by serious illness. If in any doubt,
consult your doctor. Be sure that all the eggs you use are as fresh as possible.

© Verlags- und Vertriebsgesellschaft Dort- Hagenhausen Verlag- GmbH & Co. KG, Munich, Germany
Original Title: *Das Kräuterkulinarium. Meine Kräuter – meine Lieblingsrezepte*
ISBN 978-3-86362-023-3

© for this English edition: h.f.ullmann publishing GmbH
Translation from German: Susan Ghanouni in association with First Edition Translations Ltd, Cambridge, UK
Typesetting: The Write Idea in association with First Edition Translations Ltd, Cambridge, UK
Cover design and layout: Simone Speth, Potsdam
Overall responsibility for production: h.f.ullmann publishing GmbH, Potsdam, Germany
Printed in Germany, 2016

ISBN 978-3-8480-0935-0

10 9 8 7 6 5 4 3 2 1
X IX VIII VII VI V IV III II I

www.ullmann-publishing.com
newsletter@ullmann-publishing.com
facebook.com/hfullmann
twitter.com/hfullmann_int

MIX
Paper from
responsible sources
FSC® C004592